ENLIGHTENMENT
THROUGH ORBS

Also by Diana Cooper

Ascension through Orbs (book) (with Kathy Crosswell)
Asecension through Orbs (double CD) (with Kathy Crosswell)
The Wonder of Unicorns
Unicorn Cards
A Little Light on Angels
A New Light on Ascension
A Little Light on the Spiritual Laws
Angel of Light Cards
Children's Angel Cards
Teenangel Cards
Angel Answers
Angel Inspiration
Discover Atlantis (with Shaaron Hutton)
Atlantis Cards
Wisdom Cards (with Greg Suart)
Light Up Your Life

ENLIGHTENMENT THROUGH ORBS

The Awesome Truth Revealed

by
Diana Cooper & Kathy Crosswell

FINDHORN PRESS

First published by Findhorn Press 2008
(A previous, different limited edition was published
by C&C Publishing, also in 2008)

ISBN 978-1-84409-153-9

British Library Cataloguing-in-Publication Data.
A catalogue record for this book is available from the British Library.

Edited by Michael Hawkins
Cover design by Guter Punkt & Thierry Bogliolo
Interior design by e-BookServices.com
Printed and bound in the European Union

1 2 3 4 5 6 7 8 9 10 11 12 13 14 13 12 11 10 09 08

Published by
Findhorn Press
305A The Park,
Findhorn, Forres
Scotland IV36 3TE

Tel +44(0)1309 690582
Fax +44(0)131 777 2711
eMail info@findhornpress.com
www.findhornpress.com

Dedications and Acknowledgements

Kathy would like to dedicate this book to her brother George, who was gifted spiritually and whose passion later in life was to capture Orbs in action. And also his children Elaine, Kelly, Lorna, Stephen, Jade and Saffron.

Diana would like to dedicate this book to her guide Kumeka, the angels and the unicorns with thanks for all they have taught her and for their trust in her.

We would like to thank all those who have sent us pictures of the Orbs they have photographed. With special thanks to those who have so generously allowed us to show their Orb pictures:

Prentha Naidu	Glenda Proctor
Radka Jurcgova	Johanna Pulli
Pam Raworth	Susan Clayton
Riina Lazovskaja	Lynda Hughes
Andrew Wood	Karen Yardley
Alison Relleen	Anne-Marie Bentham
Mandy Whalley	Mary Spain
Eunjung Choi	Helen Eggington
Liz House	Bernadette Gallagher
Cindy Bramhall	Jeni Floyd
Kari Palmgren	Erica Thomas
Chris and Joy Saloschin	Rosemary Stephenson

We would also like to thank Sue Stone, Author of *Love Life, Live Life,* Steve Bishop and Diana Crosswell for their generous assistance. Thierry Bogliolo, Sabine Weeke and our editor Michael Hawkins of Findhorn Press, have been most encouraging and helpful.

But most of all we thank our guides Kumeka and Wywyvsil, Archangel Michael and the great beings who have worked with us to bring *Enlightenment Through Orbs* forward.

Table of Contents

About the Authors	1
About this Book	7
Chapter 1: About Orbs	11
Chapter 2: Guardian Angels	15
Chapter 3: Children	21
Chapter 4: Angels	25
Chapter 5: Protection	29
Chapter 6: Clearance and Transmutation	35
Chapter 7: Angels of Love	39
Chapter 8: Animals	43
Chapter 9: Sound	49
Chapter 10: Spirits	55
Chapter 11: Elementals	61
Chapter 12: Guides and Masters	67
Chapter 13: Archangel Michael	73
Chapter 14: Archangel Gabriel	77
Chapter 15: Archangel Uriel	81
Chapter 16: Archangel Chamuel	85
Chapter 17: Archangels Sandalphon & Metatron	87
Chapter 18: Archangels Purlimiek, Gersisa and Butyalil	91
Chapter 19: Unicorns	95
Chapter 20: Receive energy from the Universe	99
Meditations and exercises with the Orbs to raise your Consciousness	103
How to recognise Orbs	141
Glossary of Orbs in this book	147
List of Orb photographs	153
Bibliography	157

About the Authors

Diana's Story

I met Kathy at a friend's house and we got on immediately. She was a medium and she also played table tennis; a winning combination for me! I was very busy writing *The Wonder of Unicorns* and wondering when I would ever get the time to finish it.

They say you should ask a busy person to do a project and somehow they will get it done. Our guides clearly thought so, for they got Kathy and me together and asked us to write a book on Orbs.

During that first evening they gave us information about some Orbs that we already had on photographs and we found it so fascinating and awesome that we were buzzing with excitement. I had never spoken to Kathy's guide Wywyvsil and she had not connected with Kumeka but our new connections happened very quickly.

Of course we said we would write this book. I felt privileged to be asked and indeed it has been an amazing journey for our guides, angels, archangels and even much higher beings from the angelic hierarchy have worked with us on it. I have learnt such a lot about so many things!

I have also made connections with spiritual beings I have never met before. I had no idea that the angels, archangels, fairies, elementals, unicorns, Masters, guides and other beings did so very much to help us. Their involvement with our planet and us was way beyond anything I had any concept of.

We soon realised that Orbs are waiting to show us about the spiritual realms and their interaction with us.

My Connection with Kathy

Kumeka, my spirit guide, told us that Kathy and I were biological sisters in Golden Atlantis and worked as priestesses in a temple. It was for this reason that we were brought together to do this Orb project. Kumeka added that either of us could write this book on our own but when we were together we created a higher, purer energy. We also learnt that we come from the same planet of origin, not from this universe, which was another special link.

My Connection with Kumeka

I have written in several books about my connection with my guide Kumeka, who is now the Master of the Eighth ray. He has helped me write many books and was often with me when I was talking at seminars. After I co-wrote *Discover Atlantis* with Shaaron Hutton, Kumeka withdrew. It felt very strange not to feel his presence near me.

Imagine my delight when he returned to work with me on this book! I was so pleased and, because I feel very close to him, I can receive information easily.

My Spiritual Journey

This started when I was forty-two and in despair. I was visited by an angel who changed my life. After that I dedicated my life to spiritual service and have had the most exciting and amazing journey. I have worked with angels, unicorns and the entire spiritual hierarchy and travelled world wide in my quest to serve spirit. Now our guides and angels have patiently spent hours teaching Kathy and myself about Orbs and asked us to spread enlightenment through them.

How this book was written

I am claircogniscent and mediumistic. Claircogniscence means knowing. Occasionally I am clairvoyant but mostly I just know. I guess I have become more attuned to Kumeka, the angels and unicorns over the years. As we were preparing this book Kathy and I would look at an Orb picture and ask questions. My mind would go into silence and the answer would come into it.

Kathy being clairsentient and a medium would receive the same responses in a different way. She also has the ability to go right into and through the Orbs to access cosmic information at a very deep level. We found we had different but complementary spiritual and psychic gifts and worked very well together, each bringing through parts of a whole picture, so this was a very exciting project for us both.

Many great beings of light gave us information, Archangel Michael, Serapis Bey, unicorns, Lord Kuthumi the World Teacher amongst others. The most awesome connection happened on a Saturday afternoon. Mother Mary entered to speak with us. I have worked with her many times so it was a familiar and beautiful contact. She indicated that she was paving the way for someone greater and everything went very still.

Our new telepathic connection came in very slowly as if it was hard to lower its vibration that much but gradually speeded up and soon we felt truly connected. It transpired to be a Seraphim. I said that I did not think they worked with humans and the reply was that they do not, but they work with projects of importance to humanity. We were overawed, humbled and felt a deep sense of the responsibility of this mission to spread information about the Orbs.

The Orbs

Looking into the Orbs offers healing, transformation and enlightenment. Every single one is a spiritual being and appears in a photograph to tell a story. They are quite extraordinary. I can't begin to tell you how they make me feel. Almost from the first day I saw one, they have been flashing in my third eye day and night and opening me up. With some I feel as if I am stepping into another world, others that I am being enfolded in love. One or two play with my heartstrings and are very emotional. A few are so extraordinary that I feel a sense of awe and wonder from the tips of my toes to my heart. Sometimes I feel the unicorns have jumped from the Orb and are filling me with their love, hope and light. At other times I feel as if I have the energy of an archangel round me and can sense their colours radiating around my body. It has been completely amazing.

I do hope you enjoy reading this as much as I have enjoyed working with them.

Kathy's Story

As a child I grew up in a cottage which was very active with spirit. At this time I knew I could see spirits but was quite scared. I often slept hidden under the blankets as, each night after everyone had gone to bed, I would hear footsteps climbing the stairs. A figure would enter my room and stand looking out of my window.

At this time of my spiritual development I was unable to converse with these spirits. I was helped by my mother who is also very intuitive. My brother George, to whom I have dedicated this book, was also very aware of spirit. As a child a spirit used to sit at the foot of his bed. Later in life he found this spirit to be a very good friend of his from a past life.

In my early twenties I met my husband Paul. He is a wonderful man, an amazing healer and spiritual teacher, with instinctive intuition and highly guided. We have three beautiful children who are also very intuitive and guided. Paul and I began our journey of spiritual growth and development together back in the early 1980s.

I soon realised that I was clairsentient and claircogniscent and occasionally, if I am lucky, I am clairvoyant. I feel very humbled to have been given these wonderful gifts and am pleased to share the inspiration I am given by my guides with others. I really love helping others achieve their spiritual potential and I also enjoy being a medium.

I receive so much and in so many ways from running spiritual development classes. Seeing people develop their spiritual links and skills is very rewarding. So often people lack confidence, but through some very simple fun activities they realise they are guided and that they can communicate with their guides and other beings in spirit. Every single class and group I run always leaves me feeling very lucky to be able to do this and bring so much joy to others.

My brother George was a wonderfully kind and thoughtful man. He was constantly amazed and excited by the intricate and detailed information he was given by spirit. It was always very philosophical and gave good insight into many technical and scientific topics. He was able to put things into perspective and helped to keep my feet firmly on the ground.

He came round to my home one evening, very excited as he had just brought some equipment which enabled moving Orbs to be captured. He set the equipment up and we spent a very enjoyable evening recording Orbs in every room in our house. The most surprising was when my husband Paul gave George some healing. They clustered round this activity and came so close a mist formed around both George and Paul. They still continued to circle this activity and when the healing finished they returned to their more individual movements. My brother gave me this equipment to continue capturing Orbs in action.

One evening I took this equipment to Diana's house and we were delighted by the Orbs as they came close to us. We were astonished by how they changed their movement depending on what we were doing at the time. They were beautiful.

How I Met Diana

I met Diana at our mutual friend Sue Stone's house. She is a very close friend of mine and encourages me to branch out of my comfort zone – not always an easy challenge! Diana and I got on immediately and it wasn't long after this that our guides conspired (I am sure of this) to get us together so they could invite us to write this book.

Soon Diana and I were working on this book and we were delighted when my two children in spirit appeared with Diana's aunt in one of the pictures sent to us. They had been brought to us, as they wanted me to know they were enjoying watching me get so excited by every Orb that I see and link with. It has been a wonderful, enlightening journey.

I am thrilled about working with the Orbs as they are bringing me so much joy and information. I am reminded how small and fragile my energy is in comparison to the universal energies. I am given enlightenment, encouragement and welcomed to join with the angels to help me understand why Orbs are here and why they look as they do.

My Guide Wywyvsil

My first guide was Lone Wolf who was so patient and supportive towards me. He helped me believe I communicate with spirit. Later as my energy developed and I achieved higher vibrations Lone Wolf also asked Sousimuku to support me. He was very masterful and didn't let me deviate from my path.

Then one evening I felt that all my guides had disappeared and I felt very exposed. Of course they hadn't, I was in the transition phase of being introduced to Wywyvsil. He is a mighty energy and vibrated at such a different level it took me quite a while to resonate with him. When I did I was suddenly aware that my mediumistic skills had changed.

I have been privileged to work with my guide, Wywyvsil, now for about seven years. Wywyvsil has never walked any planet and he is destined to continue in the highest realms. He works at a very high vibration and this is always a challenge to me. Luckily, I am able to tune with him quite easily, but just as easily I can miss his intricate messages when I am not in 'the zone'.

I find it very difficult to explain how we communicate as it just happens. Sometimes I get a feeling or I just know. At other times my whole body changes and Wywyvsil will enter my being and we meld. Sometimes I will go into trance. Often if I am not listening, I will get a very strong ache in my lower third eye, or I will get a sharp pain in my ear. It quickly gets my attention.

Recently, Diana and I have found out that Wywyvsil is a Power and that he is a Lord of Karma. Powers have a frequency much higher than archangels, so he is a mighty being.

As Diana and I were working on this book we were sent a picture, which we were drawn to examine. We were told this was Wywyvsil, a bright light with a tail, travelling fast to radiate love and light over Africa. It nearly brought me to tears as I could physically see his energy and I felt intensely the amount of pure love and light he was bringing to Africa. It made me really proud and very humbled to work with him.

Whenever I look into an Orb I know I am standing in its energy and I have my back to our dimension and am looking down into its depth. The layers are clearly defined and appear infinite. The colours are beyond anything I can explain. The experience is so extraordinary – I am loved, protected, special, empowered, and capable and I sense there is nothing I could not do. I come alive and I just have to tell everyone how wonderful it is to be me at this moment. This is what Orbs can do. I know this journey has only just started for me.

About this Book

Diana's Overview

Kumeka asked us to call this book *Enlightenment through Orbs* because you can be given messages and receive enlightenment simply by looking at them. The pictures retain the light of the angelic beings and this contains spiritual information and knowledge.

This means that through the Orb photographs you receive energy directly from the angels, archangels, unicorns and others of the spiritual hierarchy. It will enter your consciousness whether you are open to it or not and start to prepare you for greater enlightenment. If you are already aware and consciously ready to receive the energy, it really can affect you at a deep level.

Every Orb is the visible manifestation of a spiritual being that radiates a message or energy or both. Many of those in this book are a merging of two or more angels or masters and these often offer enhanced information and light.

The large Orb on the front cover contains the energies of Archangel Gabriel, with a unicorn and spirits as do the two Orbs at the bottom of the picture. The white Orb is Archangel Gabriel with an angel of love. On the right is one of Archangel Gabriel's angels with spirits, while the smaller blue Orb on the right is an angel with a spirit and Archangel Michael's energy.

These Orbs are bringing you greater enlightenment and clarity about your path.

When I complained to Kumeka that I was so busy working on the book that I had no time for meditation, he replied that looking at the Orbs had a similar effect and for some people was a much more effective path to spiritual growth. My meditations are sometimes all over the place, so I was delighted!

Some pictures contain Orbs of different spiritual beings. Each will have a separate impact on you but together they give you an even greater opportunity for enlightenment. Every Orb tells a story. A few pictures taken sequentially paint a progressive picture of the spiritual world.

An Orb is a key to your consciousness so each time you look at a picture you will, at some level, receive a spiritual download. Even if your mind is closed to the divine planes, their energy will reach you. For those who are awake and aware, the messages and energies radiated by the Orbs can affect you profoundly.

With each photograph I tell you exactly what messages you can pick up and what energies you can receive from each picture. By using this book you can accelerate your spiritual journey and expand your enlightenment.

How To Use This Book

I suggest you read through and look carefully at the photographs. You may be particularly drawn to some pictures or you may decide that you need certain qualities or energies radiated by various Orbs. In this case it would help you to sit quietly and examine them. Make a list of these and go back to experience them. The more you do this, the more of their spiritual light you will access. The following meditation practice may help you to settle your mind before you work with the pictures.

Meditation

Meditation is about quietening your mind so that you can receive a greater quantity or quality of the energy you want. Here is an exercise which will enable you to draw from the Orbs more of the frequency that you need. Remember that the spiritual beings will be working with you as you do this.

1. Find a place where you will be quiet and undisturbed.
2. Light a candle to raise the vibration.
3. Sit or lie.
4. Take a few minutes to look at your Orb picture. It may help you to soften your eyes or narrow your eyelids when you do this.
5. When you are ready, close your eyes and relax.
6. Focus on your breathing, counting to four on the in breath and six on the out breath. Do this until you feel your mind becoming quieter. If you are experienced at meditation, you can use any means you find appropriate.
7. You may want to conjure up the picture of the Orb in your mind's eye but if you do not wish to do this, that is also fine.
8. Allow any thoughts or feelings to come up for you.
9. If you find yourself connecting with the spiritual beings in the Orb you may receive a message or insight.
10. You may want to ask a question.
11. When you have finished open your eyes and thank the beings who have been with you.
12. Some people like to keep a journal and note down their experiences.

Exercises, Prayers or Visualisations

There are meditations, Prayers or Visualisations for each Orb to enhance their energy for you and to help you assimilate their light.

Advanced Meditation with the Orbs

Kathy has prepared a series of meditations which have been given to her by her guide Wywyvsil for this book.

How to Recognise Orbs

Each Orb has a signature which can be recognised and we give some 'signposts' to help you identify them. Remember though, to let your own intuition tell you who they are.

Glossary

There is a little about each angel, elemental, guide, Master or other spiritual being mentioned in this book in the glossary.

Chapter One

About Orbs

Why are Orbs appearing?

Humans can only see and hear within a specific frequency band. Angels and other beings of light vibrate on a different frequency and because many people only believe in that which is tangible, the masses are denying the existence of the spiritual or are oblivious of it. Because of this, much of the help that is available to them is lost and huge numbers of individuals are confused and without hope.

People want proof of the existence of a spiritual world. For centuries the spiritual hierarchy has tried to draw people's attention to the dimension beyond our normal senses and various methods have been tried. For example, at one time ectoplasm, a visible emanation of spirit, was created, but this takes energy and appears in limited conditions, so people were very sceptical of it. It was time for some new proof to emerge.

The angels and Masters in charge of the project chose the appearance of Orbs in photographs as a physical demonstration of spirit because they arouse people's interest and cause them to question. In addition, every time someone sees an Orb the angels have a chance to touch that person while they are alert, curious and open to possibilities. Naturally, the angel connects with them anyway, but if their mind is closed or unconscious, it does not have the same impact.

Were angels and guides instrumental in developing technology to capture the Orbs on film?

Yes they were, but the consciousness of the people who developed this technology was important. The angels and higher guides took the opportunity to connect with these particular scientists and influence them.

Why do spiritual beings appear as Orbs or circles?

When you capture an Orb you view the energy field of the being. The light body or merkabah in which a spirit travels is usually seen as a six pointed star shape. However, as the being evolves their light body becomes a more feminine round shape. The Orb was chosen because a circle represents wholeness and completion.

In addition a globe can carry a higher frequency than other shapes, because it has no corners to restrict the flow of energy. It also encloses and protects the entity travelling within it. Finally, because they are coming through film, which is a medium that is now available to everyone, Orbs are captivating people's interest.

Why do Orbs appear in some photographs and not others?

Orbs only appear in pictures when the photographer has a certain consciousness. They must be in a fifth dimensional space, with their aura expanded. Love is the key. The mind or third eye is irrelevant. It is not about being psychic or intellectual. In order to photograph Orbs you must develop love consciousness.

Certain combinations of chakras must be open, and these are the heart, crown and feet or heart, crown and solar plexus. When the heart, crown and feet chakras are all awake the channel from God is open right through the person. When the solar plexus is open, you are reacting from instinct and this means the heart is connected.

If there are no Orbs in a picture does that mean there are no spirits in that place?

No. Spiritual beings are everywhere. It just indicates that the photographer was not in the right space or level of consciousness at the time the picture was taken. For example, there are always angels and spirits at weddings. I recently went to a beautiful wedding where the photographer was a rational, intellectual person, so no Orbs showed up in the photos. But look at picture (4) of a wedding in Finland. This, typically, shows how many angels and spirits of loved ones usually attend a celebration.

How to take Orb photographs

Just open your heart, think about the angels or elementals and ask them to come into your photograph. You may be surprised.

Can you make false spiritual Orbs?

No you cannot. A spirit Orb is a spirit Orb but human made Orbs can be falsely interpreted. I received an impassioned e-mail from a man who said he had been making Orbs appear on his photographs using dust and drops of water. He felt people could be hoodwinked into thinking they were spiritual entities and therefore no Orbs should be interpreted.

We have seen Orbs which are tricks of the light and others which are a result of dust and rain. However, these do not contain a spiritual frequency nor do they contain a message or special divine energy.

How do I know if it is a spiritual Orb?

Tune in and feel the energy. This is something you can practise and we are not saying that it is always easy or that we always get it right.

How can you tell if an Orb is active?

Most angel Orbs are witnessing and holding the energy of what is happening, therefore they are round. If they are actively radiating at that moment they change shape, either elongating, becoming concave or hexagonal.

Why are there different colours and shapes in Orbs?

There are many dimensions, all with different frequencies, and it is through these that the Orbs take form. Each angel, archangel, principality, power, spirit and elemental has its unique look and colour because of their individual purpose and their own particular vibration. Please see the section on How to recognise each Orb.

Many of the Orbs are multi-aspects of angels and archangels. These aspects are very intricate and detailed messages of enlightenment.

How is an Orb made up?

Each Orb's centre is connected to Source and brings the purest divine energy. Many Orbs are layered from their centre in concentric circles. This brings the relevant frequency from the various layers of the spirit world for the highest purpose and to enable everything to be enlightened.

The outer circle is always the circle of protection, the frequency which allows your camera to capture Orbs. Beyond the outer circle is its aura, which touches your aura, enabling you to become 'tuned' to them. This draws you to take photographs of them. Most Orbs appear flat, but they are actually varied in shape, particularly when you start to engage with them.

Do our intentions affect the messages from the Orbs?

The Orbs work in a very similar way to positive thought, the vibrations of which connect with positive responses from the Universe. Those bringing messages and energies from the Universe vibrate at a frequency matching perfectly that of the person who needs to receive them. Your intent enables the Orbs to share their messages and energy more easily.

Are there harmful Orbs?

No. Dark angels do not have a light body.

What about the faces that are seen in so many Orbs?

The Orbs also carry spirits to the heavens and to our world and these are clearly seen in them. Because spirits of those who have passed over vibrate at a frequency only a little higher then our own, it is easy for them to be seen in the Orbs.

Why do angels and elementals need to accompany spirits and Masters?

Because these spirits and Masters have experienced human emotions, their compassion might make them want to help us and interfere with our karma and life plan. The angels hold them steady and do not allow this. They only accompany those who have been incarnated; for example, Kumeka does not need this angelic protection.

The Orbs on the front cover

This is a magnificent picture of the angelic realm bathing in the sunlight. The biggest Orb and the two at the bottom of the cover are Archangel Gabriel with a unicorn, carrying spirits. The pure white Orb is Archangel Gabriel with an angel of love. To the right Archangel Gabriel is transporting spirits. The small blue one on the right is an angel with one of Archangel Michael's angels carrying a spirit. Just looking at this picture brings you purification, expanded enlightenment and protection.

The Orb on the back cover

This is a Seraphim, the highest and most awesome of the angelic hierarchy. This one was taken by Kathy and is Seraphisa who is helping to keep people relaxed and open hearted. When you look at a Seraphim Orb you make a connection with these mighty beings.

Chapter Two

Guardian Angels

Everyone has a guardian angel who is with them from birth to death. If you really need your guardian it will be very close to you, supporting you. However, if you feel relaxed and comfortable your guardian will move away and watch from a distance. This can clearly be seen on photographs where your angel appears as a pale white disc, sometimes near and sometimes far away.

In Orb pictures you can tell if a person needs support or assistance from an angel by its proximity. We were sent a picture of people dancing. The guardian angels had withdrawn from the dance floor, all except one. This was directly over one of the girls' heads. She was feeling awkward and it was beaming support to her.

Every single person has their own guardian angel who is with them throughout all their lives. Your guardian angel holds your divine blueprint. It constantly whispers to you about your highest pathway or the best way to deal with a problem or heal a relationship.

If you are in dispute with someone or angry with them your guardian angels are holding hands in perfect love for they are aware of the higher picture. They seek to help you develop friendship and harmony with everyone, so if you ask them to assist you with a reconciliation or tricky communication, they will radiate peaceful possibilities to you. If you simply cannot resolve a problem, your angel will hold for you the vision of the highest outcome, making it possible for you to achieve it.

We were sent a telling picture of some people who had not spoken for fifteen years and were now meeting to try to resolve the dispute. Their body language demonstrated their discomfort but the white Orbs of their guardian angels were very close to them. They could be clearly seen over their heads, holding the vision of reconciliation for them. Your angels will always help you to build bridges with others.

You can ask your guardian angel to intercede with someone on your behalf. For example if you deserve a raise at work but your boss does not listen, ask your guardian angel to talk to his angel about it. Remember to tell your guardian angel sensibly and rationally why you believe your services are worth more and ask him to pass this on to your manager's angel. You can ask for help to heal a friendship, support a new business, to do well at an interview or find something you have lost.

Always remember to ask your angel.

In order to listen to the guidance of your guardian angel it is necessary to quieten your mind and let their advice drop into your consciousness as thoughts. Most people are very close to their angels so the vibration of the information they give you feels very familiar, almost like your own thoughts but with a golden clarity. We call it intuition.

Because you have free will as a human being, you have to ask for the help you need and your angel will endeavour to bring it to you. Nothing is too small or too large. However, you must request something for the highest good of yourself and all others who are involved.

Your angel will not organise something for you which is not spiritually correct. A simple example of this would be if you ask for a parking space. You reach the car park and there it is waiting for you. 'Thank you angels', you say and sigh with relief and at that moment someone else nips into it. Remember that their need was greater than yours or it was not the right space for you! Trust that there is a better one for you.

You have, of course, free will to ignore the guidance of your angel. Sometimes they are busily shutting doors to prevent you from going down the wrong path in life. If you stop to listen you may learn that there is a much better opportunity being prepared for you.

Perhaps you need to gain more experience first or wait for a more complementary relationship. However, if you absolutely insist on doing it your way, the angels will yield to your free choice and let you take the route dictated by your ego. Then, in due course, they will patiently pour light onto you as you try to extricate yourself from the mess you have created.

Most of us have done it. We insist on going out with someone unsuitable, taking the job we want despite all indications that it is not right for us, watching or reading violent material, eating the wrong food and a million other things.

Our lives could be much easier and more fulfilling if we realised how much guidance and support there is for us – and listened. See the picture, number (20) in Chapter 10, where the man's unicorn, the spirit of a loved one and an angel of love are talking into his ear. We have been sent several such pictures. The spiritual worlds really do try.

Angels are androgynous as they are beyond sexuality, so they are neither male nor female but they may come with masculine or feminine energy, depending on what you need. This is why people sometimes assign gender to them.

Your guardian angel watches over you and protects you on a day-to-day basis. It works with your spirit guides to orchestrate opportunities, co-incidences, meetings and assistance for you. If you sense that someone needs help you can mentally ask their angel to look after them.

Your thoughts then create a bridge of light, which allows their angel to assist them. However angels cannot change the Divine Plan or prevent someone from having an experience their soul needs for growth.

How to recognise a guardian angel Orb

Guardian angel Orbs are usually opaque white discs which can be small or large. Sometimes, if the angelic presence is needed they are close to or on a person. When the angel's charge feels comfortable and safe the Orb may be some distance away, just watching.

How guardian angels can help

Your guardian angel has your highest interest at heart. We were sent a wonderful photograph of a couple flirting. An angel of protection had placed itself strategically between them and her guardian angel was firmly on her crotch! The message was loud and clear.

Angels support and protect

Your guardian angel will support you in any way possible. We have seen several Orb pictures where people are singing. They may think they are doing it alone but the evidence of guardian angel Orbs by their throats may persuade them otherwise. Often the Orb in the throat is supporting the voice as well as protecting the person from the vibration of the microphone or the musical instrument.

Support and protection

When you look at picture (1) you will receive courage to speak wisely and to hear with understanding

Your angel helps you in so many ways. If you are about to say something tactless, inopportune or hurtful or if you are not standing up for yourself, your angel will leap into your throat and try to help you to say the right thing or to keep quiet.

We have a brilliant example of this in picture (1) where the guardian angel Orb in the woman's throat is blurred because it is moving very quickly to support her to say wise words. When you look at this Orb it reminds you to speak in a

Photograph by Prentha Naidu

Picture 1

considered way. It also tells you to listen. We often hear our angel's voices through our throat chakras. If we do not like what we are being told we resist by tensing up the back of our neck. Then we get a stiff neck. Looking at this Orb will help you to listen.

Collecting energy for you

There are certain places where the energy is very high and pure. Most people have walked in mountains, by the sea, a waterfall or in the woods and experienced the special quality of the air. As you breathe in this prana it lifts you physically, mentally and emotionally. Whenever you visit such a location your guardian angel is with you helping to optimise your experience.

When you look at picture (2) you will receive joy and life force as well as purification and an opening of your consciousness to new opportunities.

In picture (2) taken by Glenda Procter you can see angels bringing spirits to collect prana from the waterfall, which is a high energy point. On the right is an angel of Archangels Gabriel, Uriel and Michael with spirits, watching over and protecting the area and at the same time collecting energy.

All the beings of light are gathering the life force available in order to take it back to their humans. As you explore this picture the Orbs will give you an

Picture 2

Photograph by Glenda Procter

invitation to visit a high energy point in nature to revitalise yourself. They are reminding you of the power of nature to enrich and reinvigorate your life.

Chapter Three

Children

Angels, unicorns and fairies love children and are very close to them because they retain their essence of innocence, joy, curiosity and love.

Young children are so fresh from the spirit world that they still remember their divine origins and many of them can see elementals, spirits and angels. We have been surprised at how many unicorn Orbs we have seen with small children.

Spirits who incarnate often find it very difficult to adjust to the restrictions of a body after experiencing freedom. However loving their parents, siblings and extended family, they need a great deal of support from their spiritual helpers. People often comment on babies who smile or chuckle as they evidently look at someone invisible. It could be a relative in spirit who is visiting the child or whose job it is to keep an eye on it from the spirit world, or it could be a guide or angel watching over their charge.

A friend of mine had three small boys, who were always climbing trees, racing round on skates and bikes and generally engaging in life with enthusiasm. Their mother was in despair about them but when I explained that children have guardian angels she was very thoughtful. At last she nodded and commented that she was convinced none of her little lads would have survived if they didn't have someone looking after them. When she understood that she could communicate with their guardian angels she was absolutely delighted.

It had a big impact on the family, for the mother asked their guardians to be on extra vigilant duty when the youngsters were out playing. She could then relax. She said that the number and severity of their cuts, scrapes and bruises diminished from that time. Their guardian angels and angels of protection did an excellent job!

There is an Orb picture on www.dianacooper.com of a very special enlightened child who died at the age of six. She had only incarnated for a brief time in order to teach her family and friends many lessons such as love, patience, endurance, courage and letting go.

During her short lifetime she loved the fairies who became her friends. When she died many angels arrived to conduct her spirit over and with them danced her fairy friends helping her transit. The picture shows the angel Orbs travelling with her spirit, while the tiny sparks of fairies accompany them.

Sometimes people ask why a child should have such a short challenging life and where was her guardian angel? Why was he not keeping her safe and preventing her from passing over so young? The reason is that the great oversoul of the child, who takes all the higher decisions about her incarnation, dictated that it be so. Perhaps the child only had a few lessons to learn or teach.

The guardian angel has to abide by this choice which is the free will of the soul. In that case when it is time for the child to leave their body, their angel can only hold their hand and help them to pass into the light.

When you look at picture (3) you receive the energy to work with the angels to help your child

This picture also opens people up to nurturing and compassion.

We gasped when we saw the amazing Orb in picture (3) over the children. Some children receive wonderful extra protection. In this photograph the beautiful Orb over the two little boys is a merging of angels of Archangels Michael and Uriel as well as the guardian angel of the child on the far right. Together they are beaming energy to protect this boy and hold the friendship between the two of them steady.

Picture 3

Photograph by Radka Jurcgova

There is a big unicorn Orb on the second boy. The unicorn is drawn to him because he is sensitive and wants to help people. This special Orb contains the reminder that you can call in protection for your child. Exploring it also opens you up to nurturing and compassion.

Interestingly in a second picture sent to us of the same children, the pale white Orbs of their guardian angels could be seen over each one of them. The older boy had a unicorn Orb on his head, not the same unicorn as in the previous picture but his own. There was also a fairy with them who was being playful and trying to make them laugh. It certainly demonstrates how children are looked after and cared for. You can help the angels by practising the visualisation in the section of meditations and exercises with the Orbs to raise your consciousness.

Guardian angels really do support their children in any way that is right. We were sent one photograph that appeared quite freaky at first glance as the child had an Orb right over her face. It seemed like a weird mask. When we examined it more closely we received guidance that the little girl was a psychic sensitive who had incarnated into a family who did not understand her openness to spirit.

No one had been able to explain to her or help her to develop her gifts appropriately, and because of this her guardian angel Orb placed itself over her forehead. It was trying to protect her third eye from picking up too many 'seeings' or vibrations that would upset her.

While we were examining another picture with an Orb over a small boy's eyes, we were told his guardian angel was helping him to see the situation in his family in a more loving way.

The spiritual world can help you to keep your children and family safe. Remember to put protection round your child.

Chapter Four

Angels

There are many kinds of angels who work with humans, animals and elementals. There are angels of joy, peace, grace, protection, love, communication and legions of others. You can ask angels to help you choose presents, to find belongings you have lost, to develop qualities, help you with relationships or open your heart to forgive. Here are a few examples:

Comfort

At any time of sadness, disappointment or bereavement you can be certain that many angels are with you, supporting and comforting you. In our work both Kathy and I have heard stories of people whose grief has been lifted by the appearance of an angel.

On a number of occasions astonished but delighted people have told of the devastation of bereavement, when they have woken at their darkest moments to hear angels singing. The glory of it has dissolved their pain.

One lady had been abandoned by her partner of many years. She went to her local river, beside herself with misery and sat down to watch the water. As she stared at the ripples she saw a white feather drop from the sky right into the water. She knew it was a sign and from that moment the black cloud round her lifted. Angels will find any way they can to reach out to you.

When people are depressed all the vitality and joy is sucked out of them and they can feel only grey inertia. Their connection with God seems to be lost. Of course it is never broken but only feels as if it is. Angels are then so close to you when you are open to it that they can help you to reconnect with your divine essence.

We were sent a photograph in which one of Archangel Gabriel's angels was arriving at a house to offer comfort and help to a person inside who was very sad. Many angels of protection and Archangel Michael's angels surrounded the house.

Also, little esaks, elementals who hoover up sadness and other low energies, were busily cleansing everywhere. If that sad person had only known how hard the angels were trying to lift her spirits, she might have felt quite differently.

Purification and mental release

Everyone carries some baggage for it is part of being human. We bring in the beliefs of our ancestors as well as those we absorbed in past lives.

We turn them into patterns, sometimes entrenched, repeating the same mistakes and drawing in certain types of people and situations again and again until we are ready to let them go. The beliefs create our karma, which is a teaching method by which we learn on Earth. Even if it is someone's first incarnation on this planet, they will have undertaken lessons which will be marked on their astrological charts, so that the appropriate experiences are drawn in when needed in their lives.

In addition, our souls choose our parents and families as well as the genetic codes and conditions which shape us. It is how we respond to these factors which bring about problems. In order to release this we have to purify ourselves.

Naturally the more mental baggage you can jettison, the happier you will be, the more abundance and happiness you attract and the easier your relationships and success levels become. Now at last the angels are helping us to throw away the burdens we have been carrying for so many lifetimes. It is time to learn through joy and start to move up the spiritual mountain more easily.

Angels at a wedding

When you look at picture (4) you receive the message that angels support your decisions

Angels are always present at weddings, celebrations or any kind of ceremony. Usually there are many spirits of loved ones attending with their guardian angels too, who want to add their blessings and love. They also want to experience for themselves the joy of the event. It does not matter that it is a great-great-aunt who never met the celebrants in a physical body. It is still family! Many people continue to incarnate with their soul groups.

I sometimes hear people say how sad it was that a grandmother died before her grandchild was born and never saw the baby! On a purely physical level this is so but the grandmother is sure to visit the loved one and watch it growing up. The father who never lived to see his precious daughter get married will be there in spirit, with his angel, watching with pride and joy.

In photograph (4) there is a wonderful picture of a beautiful wedding with many angels in attendance. To the left are the guardian angels of the guests. The bridegroom's guardian angel is above his head and there is a huge guardian angel, above left of the bride, with a unicorn Orb below it. They are holding her steady.

The bright Orb at the top right and those beyond it are Archangels Michael and Gabriel who have merged to bring the spirits of the families' loved ones to watch the wedding (see the faces within these Orbs). To the groom's right is an angel of commitment. There are also lots of different kinds of angels. As you look at these Orbs you get a sense of the amount of support the spiritual hierarchy gives us.

Even if you make disastrous decisions they will support you. They never judge, condemn or are impatient! For example, if you decide to take a job which is wrong for you, marry the most inappropriate person, have children with a violent partner or run away rather than face a difficult situation, they will be there for you.

Angels of Happiness

Angels love it when people are happy for joyous laughter and innocent fun is a form of gratitude to the Creator. They flock to be with you when you feel delighted with life and they absorb some of the energy to return to you later when you need it. Angels help us so very much!

I saw a wonderful photograph taken at an event where everyone was standing waving their hands in an ecstasy of exuberance. Not surprisingly the angels were there in force, touching everyone.

Chapter Five

Protection

Your guardian angel will keep you safe on a day-to-day basis. However if you need extra protection, for example if you are out on your bicycle, walking through a city centre or practising a dangerous sport, call on Archangel Michael or his angels of protection.

When you see bright blue radiating round the edge of an Orb it is your sign that Archangel Michael's energy is there guarding you.

Quite often Archangel Michael sends one of his angels to merge with another kind of angel and you will recognise this because of the blue colour. Be careful not to confuse it with Kumeka's energy which is a similar blue. The Orbs of angels of protection are milky white, rather similar to guardian angels, and have no blue tinge.

We have seen tiny ones but also enormous ones, especially those that are merged with unicorns or archangels, to protect a town.

We have been astonished at how often we have seen angels of protection Orbs on or near people, or strategically placed round a room. We have received several photographs taken in hotel bedrooms where there have been angels of protection on duty. This is because many different people use these rooms and some may have left negative thought forms or emotional sludge behind when they depart. So angels of protection arrive with you and your guardian angel to make sure that the low frequency does not impact on you.

There are nearly always angels of protection round people and especially children. They look after all animals. If you lovingly care for something, such as a beautiful antique table or a classic car, an angel of protection will be assigned to stand guard over it. After guardian angels they are the most prolific Orbs we have seen.

We humans really have no concept of how much the spiritual hierarchy try to take care of us.

Angels of protection Orbs are milky white and rather similar to those of guardian angels. However they tend to be more opaque and are often smaller.

Protecting the family

In picture (5) you can see an angel which has placed itself between the crystal and the television. It is protecting the members of the household from the energy of the programme that is on. Many films, as well as advertisements send out subliminal messages. The energy of a violent or unpleasant programme or even the daily news lingers in the room and sensitive people, especially children, take it in.

It is an excellent idea to buy a singing bowl or cymbals to play at the end of each day over the television to cleanse and transmute the negative frequencies.

When you look at picture (5) you receive protection from electrical vibrations

The crystal by the television did not have a powerful enough energy on its own to protect the family from the impact of the broadcast, so an angel arrived to support it. If you have a properly cleansed, dedicated and charged crystal of the correct kind, it may be able to protect the householders without angelic assistance.

A black tourmaline crystal absorbs the low energy and is effective to protect you from the radiations of television, computers and electrical goods. We have seen pictures in which there are Orbs protecting different parts of the body from all sorts of instruments.

Picture 5

Photograph by Pam Raworth

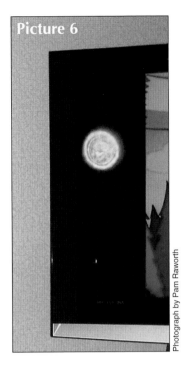

Picture 6

Photograph by Pam Raworth

When you look at the Orb number (6) you receive a feeling of love and protection

Picture (6) is an enlargement of the Orb in (5). Now you can clearly see the blue protective force which has accumulated on the side where the television is projecting its energy. This is Archangel Michael's light. Inside it you can make out the face of the grandfather as he arrives from the other side. He is coming with love to protect his beloved family and the angel conducted him here so that he could do this. It gives a warm and fuzzy feeling.

Angels Protect Nature

Many people go for a walk to blow away the cobwebs and clear their minds. Mother Earth uses the same forces to clear her energies. Spiritually, hurricanes, gales, typhoons and any winds arise when an area needs to be cleansed, especially of mental energy, people's thought forms.

The air elementals, the sylphs gather to create a force. It is very helpful to communicate with the beings of the different elements in order to mitigate or sometimes encourage their energy. For example, if a fire is out of control you want to soothe the salamanders, the fire elementals but if your kindling is damp and you would like your fire to light, you can talk to the salamanders and ask them to help your fire to burn.

Kathy and I were most intrigued to receive a picture taken in Australia of a twister. We could see the enormous power and energy as it corkscrewed through the air, picking up everything in its path. As it moved it was surrounded by angel of protection Orbs.

We assumed that they were to protect people from the havoc of the elements but no. Our guidance was that the angels of protection had arrived to help nature itself cope with the wind.

I once had a client who owned a caravan near the coast. She had learnt to ask the angels for protection and when there was a gale force wind, she called in the spiritual hierarchy to look after her home, car and caravan. A tree fell just missing her car which was on her drive. It also managed to avoid her conservatory. When she drove to the sea that weekend, every other caravan had been lifted by the wind and smashed.

Her's stood alone, firm and untouched. She said she could sense the angels round it.

The other great protection is love and the angels work with this energy. An old man used to sit in his wooden pagoda in the garden. He had built it lovingly for his wife when she was alive and they used to spend time there together quietly contemplating their garden.

Picture 7

Photograph by Susan Clayton

He lovingly tended the flowers he planted round it. When a devastating storm arose the rain lashed everything into the ground. It was as if a dome had been placed over his pagoda. The flowers and the structure itself were untouched. He was able to sit in it and survey the mess left by the rain.

Angels protect you in nature

When you look at picture (7) you receive a knowing that the angels look after you when you are out in nature

Angels don't just protect nature. They also protect you when you are out in the countryside. Photograph No. (7) illustrates this. It is a picture of Rick out walking. You can see that the path she was climbing was slippery. It is interesting to note that there is an aspect of Archangel Gabriel with her, the pure white Orb on the left hand side, half on the picture.

It is helping her to gain clarity about something and at the same time holding her thoughts in the highest and purest light. By her head her guardian angel is radiating. Whether she realised it or not she was brought to this high energy spot, so that they could work with her. At the same time angels of protection have arrived to keep her physically safe. There is one on Rick's jacket and another on the rock. When you look at this picture you really understand how much you are guided and protected.

Chapter Six

Clearance and Transmutation

If anyone in your house or work space is upset or angry, it leaves a negative energy there. Passive anger, jealousy, sulking, grief or lower thoughts affect the feeling of a building.

If you are having an event in your home or any other building it is a good idea to cleanse and clear the space beforehand. If there is to be a spiritual meeting, clearance is an important part of your preparation. When you ask them, the angels will arrive to help you.

If you take a few minutes before an event to cleanse the room and call in the angels it makes a phenomenal difference to the feeling of the space. Even the most insensitive people are aware of the change in atmosphere and, of course, the work that you do is much more powerful.

Once I arrived early at a hall where I was doing a workshop. The energy felt sticky and clammy and not really suitable for a spiritual event. I went round with joss sticks and a singing bowl, then sat in the middle of the empty space and invoked Archangels Michael, Uriel, Gabriel and Raphael. One of the helpers had come into the back of the hall and at that moment said in a loud clear voice. 'Wow! Here come the big boys!' She had felt them whooshing into the room.

Angel of a building

Every building holds the energy of each person who has entered it and all the situations that have taken place there. The feelings are retained in the wood, brick and stone. Most people sense atmospheres and know when the people who live in a house are unhappy, sick or are quarrelling. You can go into some places and shiver even though it is a warm day.

Usually there are stuck spirits there or sometimes a horrid event has occurred which has impressed itself into the ethers.

Homes, schools, factories and offices of all kinds have angels who look after them and whose task it is to radiate divine energy to try to keep the place light.

Sometimes, despite all their efforts they cannot change it, but can do so with your help. The angel of your home helps to clear the energy in it and hold it steady. If you acknowledge its presence, cleanse the rooms and raise the vibration in them you can dissolve negativity.

Do this by lighting joss sticks or candles and playing sacred music, using singing bowls or even gongs and drums. Clapping in the corners where heavy energy congregates, can break it up so that the angel of the building can transmute it.

Prayer, meditation, chanting and spiritual practices also raise the light levels and make the task of the angel of your home easier. Your intention as you do this is very important.

You can, of course, work with the angels of factories, schools, hospitals, council offices or any other buildings in the same way by cleansing the rooms and raising the frequency within them. Flowers clear energy and raise the vibration. It also helps when you visualise light entering the space and ask the angels to fill it with qualities such as peace, love and integrity.

Calling in the Christ light, which is pure unconditional love, can make an enormous difference to the energy within a building. You do not even have to be present when you do this. You can invoke it from a distance and visualise the golden light flowing in.

We were sent a series of pictures of a building being restored. In the first picture was a very bright Orb, the angel of the building and many spirits who had not yet passed and were lingering in their old haunt. Kathy and I both felt touched by icy fingers as we looked at it. It must have affected the people who worked there.

When you connect with the angel of the building, it can shield you so that you do not feel the presence of the spirits so much.

By the second picture the work had progressed and the spirits may well have moved on for none was in evidence. Now the angel of the building appeared as an Orb right above, radiating in all directions. It was clearly protecting the place and welcoming in certain people. Interestingly in this picture there were many guardian angels of the people working inside.

People generally understand that people, animals and even trees have guardians who look after them. It is good to know that buildings also have one.

Angels of Transmutation

If you take a decision to add an extension to your home, to redecorate one of the rooms or even to do a thorough spring clean, you are signalling that you are ready to change your own consciousness.

The angels assist this, so when you renovate or redecorate, angels of transmutation congregate to help clear out the old energy and prepare the space for new energies to enter. If you actively call them in, more will arrive to assist and this will also make your transition to a higher consciousness easier.

As I was thinking about this a friend phoned to say that she and her husband were in the process of clearing out their attic which had ten years of accumulated junk in it. They resolved to dispose of everything. I reminded them to call in the angels of transmutation, which they did. Later they said they could feel the presence of the angels and it helped them remain firm in their decision to clear out every single thing and not to replace it with more junk. A few days later a new opportunity arose for the husband, in other words the angels helped to draw something new and better into their lives to replace the old.

Less than a month after this another friend was engaged in the same process. She and her husband did a massive clear out but their daughter decided to go travelling in South America and arrived with all her stuff. When I visited them I could hardly get through the back door for boxes. They were more cluttered than when they started! It is true that nature abhors a vacuum. Something always comes to fill it.

Our task is to make sure that we raise our frequency, so that the new is better than the old. It is often said that clearing out the old, redecorating, extending your home or moving are the quickest ways of expanding your consciousness. Change inevitably occurs and you will receive a great deal of invisible help from the higher realms.

Clearing the space

When you wish to learn your guardian angels can help you. They absorb the information that you need and download it to you when your mind is relaxed and receptive. This is particularly important in these stressed times when many school children and students of all ages are too tense to take in the lessons. In places where students are learning about higher qualities or there is great light, the space needs to be cleansed and the angels will help you

When you look at picture (8) you receive a transmutation of fear into confidence

In picture (8) the teacher is talking about international peace and this is naturally drawing in dark forces who want to stop her, for moths are attracted to a flame. In order to protect her and transmute this dark energy, the guardian angels of those in the class have gathered around her.

They have also clustered together so that they can communicate with each other. The angels are also seeking the best way to inspire and open the students to a higher understanding of peace and harmlessness.

Picture 8

Photograph by Riina Lazovskaja

As with many of the pictures containing Orbs, angels are giving us multiple messages. We all know that no one can learn when they are stressed. In the times of Golden Atlantis when the people truly understood the workings of the human consciousness, temple classrooms were prepared which were designed for peace and quiet. Each room was painted the perfect colour for the age group of the student. Special harmonies were played to enable the brain waves of the children to relax.

Because of this the pupils could take in and understand advanced spiritual concepts, which were telepathically imparted to them. They knew then, and we are still aware, that in order to absorb information the mind must be receptive.

The angel Orbs in this photograph are helping to facilitate a tranquil frame of mind so that the students can learn more easily. These Orbs are reminding you that angels can help you to assimilate information and at the same time they can transmute any negative force.

Chapter Seven

Angels of Love

When we first looked at Orbs we found the angels of love the easiest ones to recognise because they are so pure and bright. They simply contain shining light and radiate love. Sometimes these Orbs move so quickly that they leave a trail behind them and distant ones moving through the sky look rather like comets with tails.

After seeing hundreds of these Orbs we have a sense of just how much love there is available from the universe to every single person. So many of us seem to ignore it or be oblivious to it. Yet like any other energy you can call it in and it will touch you, making you feel good.

Naturally angels of love can help you with your relationships. The commonest reason for poor bonding with partners, friends or even business colleagues is that we do not feel lovable. If your inner child took on the message when you were a baby that you were not good enough, lovable enough or special enough, you shut down part of your heart and the result is that you now limit the amount of love you let in.

This may result in feelings of jealousy, in which case you will see the world through snake-green tinted glasses – not very comfortable. Alternatively, you may experience neediness, meanness, envy, disinterest, depression, loneliness or emptiness. All these feelings arise because your inner child feels you can never get enough love and to make it worse these emotions repel love and friendship. Because we are having a human experience almost everyone has some of these feelings occasionally.

On the other hand when your heart feels full of love you radiate attractive qualities like generosity, happiness, friendliness, nurturing or empathy and you magnetise more love and friendships to you. Again most of us open our hearts at some time and know these feelings too. The angels of love can help to fill your heart centre with happiness, joy, peace and delight. There is no shortage of love – we have seen their Orbs everywhere.

Someone e-mailed me to say that she was having a difficult time with her boy friend. She looked out of the window and there were three bright Orbs. Two of them were pure and shining. One was pink. She had seen with her own eyes

Archangel Chamuel's angels with two angels of love coming to help her. It seems to us that more people are now clairvoyantly seeing Orbs than ever before.

We were sent two different pictures, one of a man and one of a woman. Both had an angel of love right by them. We were told that they were partners who were not getting on and the angels of love had gone to each of them to bind their hearts together. It was such a reminder that angels of love can help us with relationships.

A woman sent us a picture of her new husband looking out over a lake. In front of him was a brilliant angel of love Orb with a unicorn Orb above it. The Orbs were radiating pure love and he was clearly being held in their happiness.

When you look at picture (9) you will receive from the universe a certainty that love is there for you

Picture 9

Photograph by Lynda Bailey

Lynda Hughes sent us the gorgeous picture, (9), with a note that a Patagonian parrot had been living in their village for a couple of years, though they did not know where it came from. She said it was very happy there and loved spending

Picture 10

Photograph by Andrew Wood

time with their geese and chickens. The bright Orb near the goose is an angel of love. All the others are angels bringing spirits and those round the geese have an aspect of Archangels Michael or Raphael in them. The parrot is looking at its guardian angels and you can see they too have spirits with them. There are also lots of nature spirits in the grass. You can see their faces.

When you look at picture (10) you receive an understanding of the unconditional love of animals

Photograph (10) is a marvellous picture of a dog watching an angel of love zooming past him. There can be no doubt that he can see the angel and his expression says it all.

All animals, especially cats, are very psychic. They see and hear beyond the limited frequency ranges of humans. When humans hold onto resentment and hurt, it shuts out love. Animals keep their hearts open to love for they can see angels of love and spiritual beings all around and can recognise a higher perspective. They never judge others or limit their love. They do not rationalise or share out the love that they have. Their hearts are filled with empathy and compassion, which is one reason why domestic animals are so loving and caring.

Chapter Eight

Animals

All animals have spirit protection. The more evolved species have their own guardian angels. Those like small birds or fish that belong to a group soul, have one angel in charge of the flock or shoal. We have seen photographs of animals surrounded by Orbs, not just their guardian angels but angels of protection, transmutation and love as well as archangels. There are sometimes fairies and unicorns with them as well.

Because of their innocence and simplicity animals are very much loved by the spiritual world. Most domestic animals have open hearts and teach humans about patience, kindness, forgiveness, compassion, dignity, empathy and love amongst other qualities. They incarnate into their chosen families to help them, look after them and love them unconditionally. In exchange humans agree to take care of their physical needs and love them.

Service animals like cows, sheep, goats, hens, pigs or even camels are also incarnating to learn and grow. They too teach humans many advanced qualities. When each of these species first decided on Earth as their preferred planet of learning conditions were very different. There was love and respect between humans and animals. Not one of the creatures ever considered they would be treated as sub-human. They are simply on a different pathway from people. Amazingly they have, so far, patiently tolerated the inhumanity of those who farm them for profit. You can see from the few pictures in this section how the angels are assisting them.

Animals are evolving just as humans are and reincarnate again and again to learn their lessons. Each has something different to learn. Animals reincarnate with the same families over many lifetimes, especially where there is a bond of love between them and they grow spiritually together. This is why many people say that they feel they have always known their pets. The past life memories are deep inside them.

In many Orbs we have seen the spirits of animals being brought to visit their loved ones. We include a picture (11) of a grandmother coming from the spirit world to visit her granddaughter and the cat she loved. All animals including domestic animals are psychically attuned to atmospheres and the moods of people.

They are also very guided by spirit. They feel the movements of the earth and are the first to leave an area when a disaster is impending. We could learn an enormous amount from them if we watched and understood.

Dogs

Dogs are learning about devotion, love and faithfulness. They also teach their families about these qualities. It is in learning to take care of an animal that children and many adults develop caring and empathy. Canines have a masculine energy of action and they will try forcefully to stop a negative entity, a spirit who lacks love and therefore feels malicious, from trying to harm their human charge. Many people have been in a room with an animal that growls and its hackles start to rise, while looking at something they cannot see. It has seen a dark energy and is communicating its intention of fighting for its loved ones.

We saw one such picture of a dog, with his fur standing on end, which had seen an entity. Because of the presence of this dark intruder the dog was surrounded by the Orbs of unicorns, guardian angels and angels of protection. He was looking after his family and in turn the spiritual realms were watching over him.

Cats

Cats have a feminine energy so they are relaxed but watchful, graceful and loving. Like all domestic animals they may choose to reincarnate into the same families and people often feel they have a deep connection with them. Cats look after their owners so, while most people think they are taking care of their felines, in fact the cat is protecting them and their home from entities and bad energies.

Many of them are healers and offer you healing without you being aware of it. They are very psychic, much more so than most people realise. They come from Orion and have a high degree of enlightenment.

In the time of Golden Atlantis every home had a cat, which healed the family while protecting and maintaining the frequency in the household. When the energy of Atlantis started to devolve the first thing the Magi did to try to retrieve the situation was to send to Orion for more cats. However, even this was not enough to halt the downward slide.

When you look at picture (11) you will receive unconditional love for you and those you love from those in spirit

Pam sent us a delightful picture of Misty her cat being carried by her daughter. There is a bright angel of love right by her, carrying the spirit of her grandmother.

Photograph by Pam Raworth

They are surrounded by Archangel Michael's blue. The grandmother is coming to visit the cat as well as her granddaughter out of love.

In a later photograph, which unfortunately we did not have space to publish in this book, we saw the angel of love flying through the sky, returning to the seventh heaven with her grandmother's spirit.

Horses

Horses are highly evolved and beautiful creatures, which originally incarnated to support humans before there was any other form of transport. They wanted to be free and, in the times when they were valued and honoured, they were ridden bareback without bridles. They still demonstrate to us the feeling of freedom. If you see a picture of a galloping horse, his mane flying in the wind, you will access a sense of freedom, joy and energy.

This species also wanted to undertake the lessons of Earth and evolve, then ascend as they overcome the challenges. They are learning about qualities such as dignity, self worth, honour and love and are teaching these to humans.

Picture 12

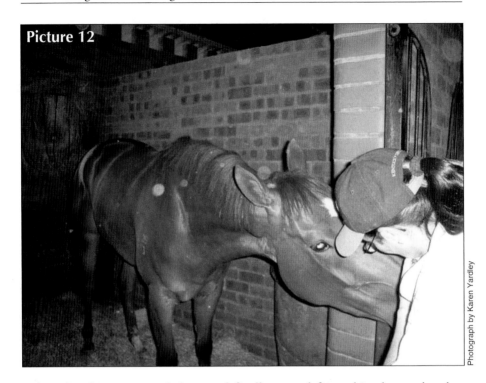

Photograph by Karen Yardley

When they have mastered these and finally ascend from this planet, they become unicorns.

Unicorns are very close to horses, as are our guardian angels to us. They can occasionally be seen galloping with a herd of wild horses. Their Orbs are often seen near their horse friends.

When you look at picture (12) you will receive a desire to connect with animals and the peace this brings

This beautiful horse, in picture (12), is called Lookalike. You can see the small Orb on her crown, which is her unicorn, opening her up to enlightenment. On the mare's shoulder and at the top left is one of Kumeka's angels bringing both enlightenment and protection. There is an angel of protection at the top centre of the photograph. The guardian angels of both horse and girl are here too. The horse's is the smaller Orb to the right, while the one at the top right is the girl's. There are also lots of tiny fairy Orbs looking like pinpricks of light. The Orbs are reminding us that there is a magical invisible world around us all the time.

When you look at picture (13) you will receive healing for your soul

If your life has been dedicated to survival, to success, to proving yourself or to amassing riches, your soul will not be satisfied. It will be wilting or weary. You

Picture 13

Photograph by Mary Spain

may even feel hurt, disappointed or insulted at a soul level. All those who have a feeling that they are not on the right path and do not know how to change, need healing for their souls.

In picture (13) taken by Mary Spain in St. George's church, she says that there is no east window, so the window effect is created entirely by the larger of the two orbs. She adds that the star underneath the Orb was made from silver paper by the children of the Sunday School! The stunning Orb to the left is of Archangels Michael, Raphael and Zadkiel merged together. The pale one to the right also contains their energies. This picture offers healing for your soul.

Some people will not like to see pictures of animals being paraded in a circus and, of course, it is time for humanity to recognise that they are all on their own soul journey and not meant for the entertainment of people. However, we wanted you to see the amount of protection that creatures are receiving from the spirit world as demonstrated in picture (14).

When you look at picture (14) you will receive a knowing that humans must expand their consciousness to honour animals

In picture (14) you can see big Orbs which contain aspects of Archangels Raphael, Uriel and Gabriel. Examine them carefully and you will be aware of green, yellow and white in them. The blue Orb is an aspect of Archangel Michael, while the one

Picture 14

Photograph by Radka Jurcgova

above the camel's humps is Kumeka merged with an angel of love, as is the one to the right above the child. One of Kumeka's angels is at the lower right and at the top right is an animal spirit being brought here by an angel merged with one of Archangel Michael's angels.

This picture reminds you that we must respect our fellow creatures. It also contains the message that you must never doubt that all animals are open to receive love and healing. It also reminds you that animals are important in their own right and are on their own path of evolution.

Chapter Nine

Sound

Fekorm

Fekorm is a Master of Music who has just arrived on Earth from another universe bringing extraordinary knowledge of the power of sound with him. He has been used to working at much higher frequencies than we are conditioned to and he has come to our planet to help us all to move to new levels.

We were told that he is on the same frequency level as an archangel and his origin is from the heart of God, like all angels. However the system in the universe he comes from is different and they do not have angels as we do. He is a Lyslih.

When he came to help Earth he studied and mastered all the ancient systems of music there have ever been on this planet. He is reintroducing the methods of healing from Atlantis, Lemuria and other ancient civilizations that we no longer have any knowledge of. At the same time he is bringing in new methods of making sound.

Certain people, like Rosemary Stephenson, who creates music with crystal bowls and her singing voice, are already attuned to his energy. She is a teacher of the Diana Cooper School and by serendipity and divine synchronicity she was in South Africa at the same time as I was in 2007. Naturally I invited Rosemary to sing at my event and everybody was delighted for she is very special. You can see the magnificent Orb of Fekorm's angel near to her as she is singing in picture (15) kindly sent to us by Alison Relleen.

This angel is healing the audience through the vibration of Rosemary's voice as she sings. On the left is a unicorn Orb supporting her. Interestingly she was on the first Teacher Training course that I facilitated after the unicorns first appeared to me to ask me to spread information about them.

It was a residential intensive taking place in France and although the course was about angels and ascension, pure white horses galloped up and down the field outside the teaching room! Everyone there made a profound connection with unicorns, including Rosemary.

Picture 15

Photograph by Alison Relleen

This picture gives you the message that angels use sound for healing, that you can receive it and that the vibration will go wherever it is appropriate, to your physical, emotional, mental or spiritual body.

When you look at picture (15) you will receive joy and healing

So many people produce lyrics and music that are attuned to the lower energies on this planet, such as melancholy, disappointment or even rage. These diminish the life force and happiness of those who hear them. Fekorm is working with the unicorns to help those who are using their creativity to inspire and encourage for the greatest good. He touches those with aspirations of magnificence and joy. One of his tasks is to teach people about the healing power of sound.

He is doing this by helping those who are ready to raise their frequency through musical vibrations by dissolving their old baggage and healing them.

In his healing quest Fekorm is also enabling those who are writing words and music that resonate with conditions such as autism, exhibited by those who cannot cope with the low frequencies on the planet. Many of us originate from other planets or even universes and there have always been many visitors on Earth.

Currently there are more here than ever before, incarnating now to teach higher qualities and enlightenment and to experience the massive opportunities available for spiritual growth. Many resonate on different frequencies from the average person and this can make life very difficult.

Also, millions do not understand the way Earth works, with its attitudes of violence and selfishness, so the vibrations of sound soothe and comfort them, reminding them there is another way. Some music reminds them of their homeland and comforts them. It is also hoped that music will help attune them to the higher frequencies available on Earth so that they can cope.

Fekorm encourages free expression and is teaching the understanding that dancing, chanting and other forms of sound work bring about the free expression that raises the frequency.

New technology and updated instruments are offering ways of producing different sounds and Fekorm is helping to bring through new ones. It is important to listen to him if you are a composer of any sort, for this will be an opportunity to spread mass healing and enlightenment in the future. However, the Master is also taking the old, such as Native American Indian drumming or Aborigine didgeridoos and is merging them with the new. By doing this he is forming them into something greater than either.

The entire human auditory range is being extended and expanded. Fekorm is working to help us hear the angelic sounds emitted by the Orbs. We will also be able to listen to the music of the spheres.

Picture (16) was taken by Pam Raworth at Angel Awareness Day in Bournemouth in 2007. Diane Egby Edwards, who is also attuned to Fekorm's energy and works with a didgeridoo, flutes and the gong, treated everyone to a gong bath during the final ceremony. To our fascination, photographs taken earlier in the day showed a big Orb of Archangel Michael merged with Kumeka over my head. Clearly they were communicating through me and protecting me.

After Diane Egby Edwards gave her awesome gong bath, Kumeka and Archangel Michael separated. Kumeka went into the audience to help people there, while Archangel Michael moved in front of the gong to protect its energy from the neediness of some of those in the audience. Archangel Zadkiel's violet energy can also been seen round his Orb transmuting any lower energies sent towards it.

At the top of the gong can be seen Fekorm, who is being guarded by Archangel Michael's blue. A spirit with its angel and also surrounded by blue can clearly be seen at the bottom of the gong. His angel has brought him to experience the sound vibrations. There are other spirits round the instrument who have also gathered to receive the frequency.

Picture 16

Photograph by Pam Raworth

Several other photographs taken at this time by different people show masses of guardian angels coming forward to absorb energy from the gong vibration to take back to their charges.

When you look at picture (16) you will receive protection and an understanding of the awesome power of sound

Most people are aware how music can change their state of mind and we had a lovely reminder of this when we were sent a photograph of a piano. The player had evidently recently risen from the stool and walked away. An angel of love was moving very quickly from the piano towards the cameraman in order to enfold them in love and bring the happiness of the music to them. It was a reminder that music can open you up to happiness.

We had never realised that angels literally collect the vibration of sound to take it to help and heal other people. However, many pictures of Orbs demonstrating this have drawn this to our attention. So if you are ever playing an instrument or even listening to a CD of beautiful music you can ask the angels to take the energy of the music to inspire, console, realign or retune others and fill them with happiness.

We were sent a series of pictures taken by Pam Raworth when she went to a concert. In them you could see spirits being escorted by their guardian angels to help those who were playing in the orchestra. When we enlarged the pictures we could see their faces in the Orbs.

These particular spirits were all musical people who have now passed over but who themselves played in orchestras during their lives. They were coming to infuse the players with extra life force and vitality and you could pick this energy up from the photograph.

Sometimes we have seen the spirits of those who loved music and still want to enjoy it being taken to musical events. Their spirits continue to receive healing and peace from listening to the sounds. Still other Orb pictures have shown angels bringing loved ones to listen to their children, grandchildren, great grandchildren and other relatives playing in concerts. The Orb pictures demonstrate to us how very much those who have passed love us and participate in our lives.

If you ever go to a children's play or concert you can be absolutely certain that the hall and especially the stage will be full of loved ones as well as angels of every description, unicorns and often a few fairies. The spirit world loves both children and music.

Chapter Ten

Spirits

When you travel out of your physical body in your sleep you are moving in your spirit body. You may then appear as a spirit Orb in someone's photograph. I was intrigued when I was told why a spirit who showed up in a picture we were sent, was taking a particular journey.

Kumeka described the person's character to me and I immediately asked if it was a certain friend of mine. My guide confirmed that it was indeed this friend and that he was being taken at night to learn a specific lesson in humility.

The spirits of those who have died live in the spiritual dimension. Here they continue to evolve until they move to a different planet for new experiences or return to this one for another incarnation. Wherever they are they enjoy visiting their loved ones and an angel always conducts them on their journey. Very rarely does the person they are coming to see know that they are there. A few people are psychic, so that they are aware of their visitor.

Occasionally spirit visitors are able to announce their presence by making lights flicker, opening a door or even turning the television or radio on. You may see that your pet is quite tranquil but watching something in the room, which could be a loved one or an angel or both. People sometimes get a whiff of the tobacco their deceased father used or a nuance of their grandmother's perfume as they pass. At other times you may sense someone's presence with you and feel comforted by it.

In the hundreds of Orb pictures we have examined we have seen the spirits of those who have passed over. Some have been earth bound and we have helped them to the light. Most are meeting up with their friends and family still on Earth, either to help them or to bring love. Some come to visit places where they were happy while they lived. Others are journeying to learn something or to enjoy the experiences offered on our amazing planet.

Spirits travel to our educational establishments to learn alongside the physical students. If they are interested in medicine they attend hospitals or if they are artists they congregate in art galleries. We saw one photograph of hundreds of spirits being taken to receive enlightenment. They were conducted by angels, archangels and the Masters who were going to teach them.

Nothing we do while we are on Earth is ever wasted for we continue our learning and interests after we have passed, as well as our quest for enlightenment and ascension.

When people pass over they love to keep an eye on new members of the family and see how they are getting on. They would have known them in the spirit world and want to continue the connection, so they come to visit when they can.

There are some people who find it difficult to release their loved one after they die. Their grief is such that they cannot enjoy their lives any longer. This is miserable for them but it is also very sad for the being on the other side who is watching and being held back.

Orb (17) contains multiple messages. Amongst them it gives the person who is finding difficulty adjusting to life without a loved one permission to start living again.

When you look at picture (17) it opens you to receive permission from those in spirit to get on with life

We were delighted to receive a beautiful photograph, see picture (17), from Ann-Marie Bentham, of her baby with its grandfather in which you can see two

Picture 17

Photograph by Anne-Marie Bentham

Picture 18

Photograph by Eunjung Choi

Orbs. In the larger one Archangel Gabriel's angel is bringing two loved ones to visit the infant. The smaller Orb is one of Archangel Gabriel's angels with a loved one and a unicorn. It is another reminder of how often there is unicorn energy round babies and children.

Opportunity

When you look at photograph (18) you receive a direct unicorn connection

In the first version of this book, published by C& C Publishing, we showed a photograph taken while I was talking in Cape Town, South Africa. You could see a big Orb behind me of my guardian angel but on the other side was a large unicorn Orb with a trail of light below it. Taking the opportunity to drink in this energy was a spirit, brought by his angel, while a second spirit was arriving to do the same.

We laughed when we saw it and the picture invited you to accept all opportunities for spiritual growth. However it did not really come out clearly enough, so we have chosen a magnificent unicorn Orb for picture (18) sent to us by Eunjung Choi. It was taken in front of the Horus statue at the Edfu temple in Egypt when they had just finished communing with Horus.

The Orb is a unicorn with an angel of love and Archangel Michael and when you explore it, it helps you make a connection to the unicorns.

Picture 19

Photograph by Mandy Whalley

When you look at picture (19) you receive love and healing for yourself and a knowing that your loved ones are receiving it too

When you go with love in your heart to place flowers on someone's grave, you call forth a great force of love and it gives your friends and relatives who have passed over the opportunity and energy to reach you. In doing so, both parties can exchange love.

It is no wonder that some people feel such a sense of peace when they sit quietly by their dear one's grave and think of them. Much is unleashed at a spiritual level.

A cluster of breathtaking Orbs arrived from Mandy Whalley, all quite different but each one astonishing. For this book we chose picture (19) which is totally awesome, in which you see a huge orange ball of light zooming with a great trail of energy. It was moving towards Mandy's grandmother's grave where she had just placed flowers. The orange ball is Archangel Metatron, full of loved ones and we were told that one of them was her grandmother.

When Mandy went with love to the grave it enabled those in spirit who cared for her to come and collect the love for themselves and to give it to Mandy. The orange Orb is travelling to make the connection. In this picture you can also see the spirit of the tree in the mid-left.

Picture 20

Photograph by Cindy Bramhall

When you look at picture (20) you receive love, protection and enlightenment

Picture (20) was sent to us by Cindy Bramhall who was living in Bahrain in the Middle East, when her family came to visit her from South Africa. She clicked this picture during a family barbeque and you can see a wonderful picture of an angel of love with a unicorn and the spirit of a loved one talking into the man's ear.

Chapter Eleven

Elementals

Elementals are the spirits of air, earth, water and fire who look after the natural world. There are fairies, imps, gnomes, goblins, elves, fauns, salamanders, undines, mermaids and so on. They are called elementals because they are ethereal, invisible to most humans and do not have all five elements in their make up. The elements are earth, air, fire, water and ether. We have seen a number of elementals in the Orb photographs which we have been sent.

Fairies are of the element air and are very bright lights that tend the flowers. They are delightful, pure, innocent, playful creatures. I have heard many stories of fairies that mischievously untie your shoelaces or hide the implement you are working with and they do love to play and tease, though they are never malicious.

However, in the work Kathy and I are doing with the Orbs we have learnt that they are much more responsible and powerful than we had any idea of. When the unicorns have purified an area with their incredible light, it is the fairies who absorb this light and then remain to hold it steady when the unicorns have moved on. They appear as bright pinpricks.

Sylphs are tiny little air spirits who work with flowers and plants like the fairies. They clear pollution round plants so to help them be healthy. Mostly they love to fly with the wind. One lady told us she had been for a lovely bracing walk while on holiday. She took a photograph of her room when she returned and sent it to us. There were tiny Orbs of sylphs continuing the clearance indoors, looking bigger than fairy Orbs but not as bright. You can call in the sylphs to help you cleanse your aura and clear the cobwebs from your mind.

Esaks are new to the Earth. They have been invited here recently to help with the cleansing of the planet at this time of change. They come from a different universe and are delighted to have this opportunity for experience, service and learning. Their task is to vacuum up negative energy, in order to prepare the area for higher frequencies coming in.

We have seen huge numbers of these in photographs. They usually but not always appear at the bottom of the picture, near the earth. Because they are so small they are like slightly smudged pinpricks, smaller than fairies.

Like esaks, the kyhils have arrived as visitors to our planet recently from another universe. Their task is to cleanse negative energy in the waters of the world. It was Archangels Purlimiek and Butyalil together who invited the esaks, kyhils and other elementals into the planet. Some are here to help clear and cleanse; others to observe how Earth operates.

Pixies never stay in a place long. They are troubleshooters, helping people with the quality of the soil and working to prevent its erosion. Their Orbs are quite distinct, small and clearly formed, often blue tinted.

Love the elementals

When you look at picture (21) you receive a feeling of empathy with the elementals

I took picture (21) in my back garden. There are always angels of love and fairies when I take pictures out there so I found it difficult to pick one out. I chose this particular photograph because the angel of love is radiating blue protection to pixies and fairies who are in the pine tree. There is a hazel cluster behind

Picture 21

Photograph by Diana Cooper

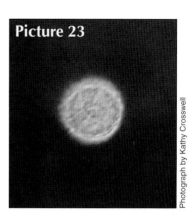

Photograph by Kathy Crosswell

the pine and the two trees are always full of life. Squirrels play up and down them, while woodpeckers, tree creepers, wood pigeons, tits, sparrows, wrens, blackbirds and thrushes love them, so it feels as if it is a place very in tune with nature.

When you love and tend your garden, by calling in the fairies and the angels, you can create a little fairyland. There is magic here.

Nature's protection

When you look at both pictures (22) and (23) you will receive energy from the nature kingdoms

When you love nature it protects you. We were sent pictures taken a few minutes apart. In the first one a truck is surrounded by a snowstorm of Orbs who are moving with it including angels, archangels and many different elementals. In the next picture the truck had arrived safely home and most of the spiritual escort had dispersed. However, a large angel of protection remained on the tyre of the truck. Kumeka told us that the truck had a slow puncture which was why the vehicle and its driver were being escorted by the spiritual world!

Kathy and I were replacing some Orbs in edition 1 of this book with new ones and as usual there were publishing deadlines. We needed new photographs of Kumeka, Archangels Gersisa, Butyalil and a Seraphim. Kumeka told us that if we went to a local portal he would appear for us, so we obediently met in this isolated spot and snapped away for a couple of hours.

It was very beautiful as the sun set, but there were no Orbs of any note. At last I decided I had had enough, so I left feeling annoyed with Kumeka. Kathy too felt disgruntled. She sat in her car and gave spirit a piece of her mind, which is something she rarely does. Then she stuck her arm out of the car window and clicked away without looking.

It was only when she arrived home that she examined the pictures. She had captured several pictures of Kumeka as well as Archangels Gersisa and Butyalil! Not only that, there was a magnificent seraphim, Seraphisa who is on the back cover of this book! We were later told that her outburst relaxed her and enabled the Orbs to come in.

When we first started taking Orb photographs I captured several of her guide Wywyvsil. At that time she felt exactly as I now did about her filming Kumeka! That's our human bit. So we asked why we had not photographed our own guides and were told we were too emotionally attached.

Out in the heart of nature Orb (22) was taken of Archangels Gabriel, a unicorn and spirits. As you look at it you receive energy from nature and a feeling of being enfolded by the natural world.

In picture (23) Archangels Gersisa and Butyalil plus three Ascended Masters, Quan Yin, Thoth and Lone Wolf are making a connection with you. Archangel Gersisa is opening you to the feminine energy of Mother Earth while Archangel Butyalil is bringing through the cosmic connections for this planet. Quan Yin is helping you to open your heart to nature. Thoth, with his strong masculine life force, is bringing forward the power and strength of nature so that you know of its ability to look after you.

Lone Wolf, the Ascended Master and spirit guide is showing you how important your connection with the natural world is. As we were talking about this a guide called Dances with Wolves connected with Kathy. He said he was a Native American Indian, very closely connected with Lone Wolf, who worked extensively with angels during his lifetime to find the right place to camp or swim. Their tribal link with angels was so strong that the great beings offered them safety and protection. They also helped them with their links to nature and to bring through their wise ancestors.

Just looking at these pictures reminds you that there is so much protection and energy available from the nature kingdoms.

When you look at picture (24) you experience oneness with nature and the elemental kingdom

Some people are able to merge with nature and belong amongst the trees and elementals. Oneness with nature was the great quality so valued by the people of Golden Atlantis for it enabled them to keep up their fifth dimensional frequency and maintain connection with Source. It is time now to bring back this knowing.

Picture (24) is a close up of an Orb taken in a garden. It holds the qualities of nature and looking at it will help you experience the oneness. In it there is

Picture 24

Photograph by Helen Eggington

an angel of love with Archangels Metatron and Michael. The message of this photograph is that nature loves you.

Chapter Twelve

Guides and Masters

We are living in an age which is preparing for enlightenment and ascension both at an individual and planetary level. Those of us who have incarnated now are being presented with the greatest opportunity for spiritual growth that there has ever been. If you accept all the help that is on offer from the angelic kingdom and the Masters of Light, your soul will make huge progress.

What is enlightenment?

Enlightenment is a state of being in which the consciousness expands to include higher understandings. It can take place in stages and you can sometimes receive sudden illumination about a subject, which enables you to embrace higher concepts. Really it enables you to carry more light, so that you can transcend lower limitations, control body functions and take power over your life. Looking at these Orbs and opening to their messages and the energies they impart is an excellent way to move forward.

What is ascension?

Ascension is a state of doing. It entails actively drawing down more of the light of your soul and monad into your physical body. This raises your consciousness and expands your spiritual awareness. It can enable physical changes to take place.

Spirit Guides

Everybody has at least one spirit guide who is attracted to their energy in order to help them. Most people have several. The more light you radiate the higher frequency the guides who come to assist you. As you evolve you attract higher guides. You may have one guide who helps you with finance, another who is a nun, a third who is very wise, a fourth who is an artist and so on. Some guides stay with you for a long time. Others are specialists who help you with a project or a particular venture.

Most spirit guides are those who have become wise on Earth while in a body. After they pass over they train to become a guide to a human. This is considered to be a very specialist task and senior guides undergo rigorous training in the inner planes.

Kumeka

My main guide Kumeka comes from another universe and has never incarnated on Earth. This means that he does not understand the limitations of being in a physical body and has very high expectations of what can be achieved! He is Chohan or Master of the eighth Ray. Kumeka has not always been with me, connecting fully about ten years ago.

He also left and watched from a distance while I wrote *Angel Answers* and *The Wonder of Unicorns*. When those projects were finished he returned for this book on *Enlightenment through Orbs*. Luckily I have several other guides who assist me as well as the angels, archangels and unicorns.

Kumeka, Lord of Light, is a mighty Ascended Master of another universe, where he has mastered all the lessons. When he first came into the Orbit of Earth he channelled only through me and Shaaron Hutton. Now however, he can touch ten million people at a time and in some Orb pictures we have literally seen hundreds of aspects of him, with his angels.

In such pictures he is transmuting negative energy in a place which has been polluted by the thoughts and emotions of humans and is then helping to raise the light levels of that area. He protects those he works with, transmutes their lower energies and touches them with enlightenment.

Kumeka is the master of the eighth ray, the colour of blue topaz, which is helping to bring about deep transmutation on our planet. This is enabling huge changes to take place everywhere. He is working closely with the unicorns, who add great light to people and situations, so together they illuminate and expand people's consciousness.

Kumeka's Orbs are blue and a very distinctive shape, bulging out on one side. This is because he is actively pushing out and directing his powerful force. This also allows people to draw more of his energy from him. Where there is negative or dark energy, people are able to pull his light to them without even asking. In contrast most of the angel Orbs are static, observing and holding the light. They change shape when active.

Kumeka works very closely with all the archangels and higher beings and his Orb is often seen merged with them. By combining their energies they can emit a more potent force for change.

Wywyvsil

Kathy's main guide is Wywyvsil and he has worked with her in 101 previous lives in various planets and universes. He has also worked with me many times. He and Kumeka are very connected and like Kumeka he has come from a different universe and has now arrived to assist humanity. He is of the angelic hierarchy, being a Power.

The Powers are a rank of angel above the Principalities and archangels. In this level are the Lords of Karma and Angels of Birth and Death. Wywyvsil is a Lord of Karma, in charge of many of the teaching schools in the inner planes, and an Angel of Birth, supervising those who are allowed to incarnate. He also works with Source and the Seraphim to help creation. He is a mighty being.

In the time of Golden Atlantis the High Priests and Priestesses and many of the highly evolved beings who were instrumental in setting up the great experiment, placed part of their energy into a great Pool of Energy, so that people could access it for their physical and spiritual needs. It contained the original pure Reiki energy. Wywyvsil is using this great Pool of Energy to send healing, transformation and enlightenment directly to Earth, so that all can access it as they did in Golden Atlantis.

The Orbs of the angelic hierarchy are keys to accessing this Pool of Energy.

Wywyvsil assisted Serapis Bey and the Seraphim to oversee the building of the pyramids after the fall of Atlantis and is very involved with healing through the Egyptian connection. The beings on the planets Sirius, the Pleiades and Orion send healing and enlightenment to Earth through the antennae of the Great Pyramid. This has now moved slightly off axis so that the signal is not as clear as it used to be and he is working tirelessly to help Earth to reconnect so that she can find her rightful place in the universe again.

Wywyvsil is very involved with healing through the Egyptian connection and continues to oversee the schools of healing and enlightenment on Earth connected to them.

He and Kumeka work with the Diana Cooper School to spread transformation, an understanding of the angelic hierarchy, the wisdom of Golden Atlantis and ascension.

How spirit guides help

While angels hold your life plan and save your life *in extremis*, guides assist you with your projects, help you to meet the right people and open doors for you. They give you specific information if you need it and work very closely with your guardian angel.

Picture 25

Photograph by Pam Raworth

Spirit helpers

These are usually but not always the spirits of loved ones who want to help you from the other side but are not qualified as guides.

Merging with Archangels

When you look at picture (25) you receive a sense of welcome and belonging on the spiritual path to enlightenment

As we have discovered from the Orbs, your guide can merge with an angel or archangel when it is necessary to radiate a particularly powerful message.

Picture (25) was taken by Pam Raworth in Bournemouth at the annual Angel Awareness Day event in 2007 where I was speaking. You can see that over my head is a magnificent Orb of Kumeka, my spirit guide, who has merged with Archangel Michael, who is my overlighting archangel. You can tell that they are working together by the bright blue band round the edge of the Orb.

Some of the other Orbs are angels who are gathering energy from the hall and taking it to the soul of someone to whom the seminar has sent healing. There are also healing angels here for people at the event. In addition there are angels of love, peace, communication, joy, transformation, enlightenment, protection, hope and purification in this picture.

You can pick up healing energy as you look at the healing Orb. It also contains the message that our guides and angels are proud to work with us. They are helping us on our pathway and we are reminded that all we have to do is ask and the assistance will come.

When you look at the Orb in picture (26) you automatically receive encouragement on your spiritual path

The next picture (26) is a close up of the Orb above my head – Kumeka, my guide, merged with Archangel Michael. They are sending healing through expansion of consciousness. At the same time they are giving answers to questions, not only through me as the speaker, but directly into the consciousness of the people in the audience. This is a very important Orb, for you can continue to pick up answers by looking at the picture of it and also link into Archangel Michael for protection. It reminds you that the answers are already in your consciousness and looking into this Orb will enable you to access them safely and confidently.

There was a time when I used to feel exhausted after talking to a few hundred people. The reason was that they were all pulling the answers to their questions from my mind. They were also drawing energy from me through my third eye. Working with Kumeka and Archangel Michael changed that, for people can

Picture 26

Photograph by Pam Raworth

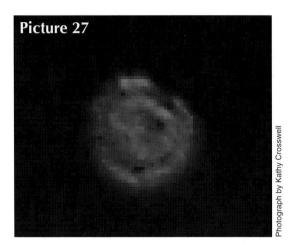

Picture 27

Photograph by Kathy Crosswell

access all that they need directly from these higher beings. This picture clearly illustrates how you can link in to the Orb.

When you look at picture (27) you receive a knowing of enlightenment NOW and assurance you are on your path

Because Kumeka has such a distinctive shape and is seen in so many photographs of Orbs we want to show you a typical aspect of him. In picture (27) you can see his colour and the essence of his being. He is the most active of all the Illumined Ones and is constantly radiating out energy where it is needed.

When you tune into his Orb you receive light which expands your consciousness and opens you to higher awareness. He also helps you affect deep transmutation on all your life issues. Remember that he will only work on you to the level with which you can cope and he can heal you by holding you in the light.

Chapter Thirteen

Archangel Michael

Archangel Michael is the protector. He carries the Sword of Truth in his right hand, a Shield of Protection in his left and wears a deep blue cloak of protection. He will always respond to a call for help by sending one of his angels. You have to do your part by asking for help and trusting that it will come.

Archangel Michael's cloak of protection.

You can ask Archangel Michael to place his deep blue cloak over you if you need your energies to be protected. It is a wise thing to do if you are about to meditate, pray or do any kind of spiritual or psychic work.

Your aura is your protective shield and these activities open it up so that lower energies or beings can enter it. For example a cloud of sticky jealousy or smouldering anger may have been left lying around by someone and if you are unprotected it can jump into your aura and make you feel jealous or angry.

If you are psychically sensitive it is always sensible to place his blue cloak of protection round you before you go out. Many people routinely visualise Archangel Michael's blue enfolding them when they rise in the morning and go to bed at night. Then they know that their aura is safe. Remember to ask for it and visualise it for your children too.

How to ask for Archangel Michael's blue cloak to protect you

Think or say aloud, 'I now ask Archangel Michael to place his deep blue cloak of protection round me.' Then, and this is most important, visualise the angels placing it over you. Picture it being zipped up from your feet to your chin. Then imagine the hood being pulled up over your head and down over your forehead or third eye. This ensures that every chakra is safe. This prayer does not work if said by rote. Your input by picturing the angels placing it on you helps to activate the protection.

What you can ask Archangel Michael to do for you

Archangel Michael will respond to calls for help. It is good to get into the habit of protecting your journey by asking Archangel Michael to be with you and then to thank him when you have safely reached the other end. You can ask him to look after your house when you go away or even during each day and night. You can ask him to protect your family and keep them safe. If ever you feel vulnerable call in Archangel Michael and he will send one of his own angels or an angel of protection to you.

I know a teenager who was jumped on by a big man in the dark. He put his hand over her mouth and was carrying her off. Luckily she was attuned to Archangel Michael so she immediately sent out a silent call to him to help her. The man suddenly and unexpectedly dropped her and ran off, leaving her shaken but unharmed – and very grateful to Archangel Michael.

Protect your journey

One January day I was leaving a friend's house after midnight. It was freezing and rain had turned to ice so I sat in the car for a few moments before I started the engine and fervently asked Archangel Michael to protect me, the car and the journey home.

Picture 28

Photograph by Patricia Haasbroek

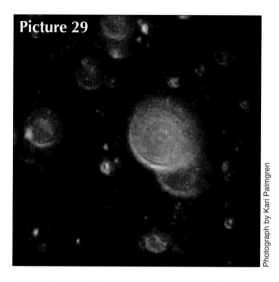

Picture 29

Photograph by Kari Palmgren

Instantly I saw his glorious blue light literally glowing and shimmering on the road in front of me. It lasted for a few minutes as I drove through the night, then faded but I knew without a shadow of doubt that Archangel Michael was protecting me.

Whenever I see a young person on a motorbike I immediately ask Archangel Michael to send his angels of protection to them and picture him enfolding the youngsters.

We were sent this superb photograph of Jason, who is 22, on his magnificent motorbike with his aunt Susan. His mother is always concerned that he will get hurt. Someone has been sending out prayers for him for picture (28) clearly shows just how much protection is being given to him!

When you look at picture (28) you receive protection from Archangel Michael

There is massive protection indicated in this photograph – a big Orb of Archangel Michael in front of the bike and a smaller one behind – also lots of little Orbs of Archangel Michael's angels. Above the young woman is her guardian angel which has streaked in to be close to her. There are also spirits at the lower part of the photograph who are attracted to the energy of the bike.

When you look at picture (29) you receive an awakening to higher powers and protection

Picture (29) is absolutely incredible. When I first saw it, it buzzed in my third eye for hours! This is Archangel Michael himself in all his glory. The blue is radiant. The light is amazing.

Chapter Fourteen

Archangel Gabriel

Archangel Gabriel always appears as a pure white column of light and this is translated into a radiant white Orb. His other half is Hope, so wherever you see an Orb of Archangel Gabriel you will unconsciously receive hope. His qualities are joy, clarity and purity and his materialised energy on Earth, the diamond, symbolises an eternity of true love. He helps you to come through change easily, so at this time of transformation he and his angels are everywhere.

Archangel Gabriel purifies people and the land and we have been astonished at how many of his angels we have seen in some of the photographs. Naturally he works closely with Kumeka who transmutes lower energies in a place or person, then Archangel Gabriel is able to purify and raise the light. He and Kumeka together help to bring enlightenment to the people there.

When your heart chakra vibrates at a fifth dimensional frequency it becomes pure white, contains the Christ light and resonates with Archangel Gabriel as well as with Archangel Chamuel.

This is Archangel Gabriel

When you look at the Orb in picture (30) you receive another level of enlightenment

Take your time to explore the bright Orb of Archangel Gabriel in picture (30) and some of the qualities of purity, clarity, joy and healing that he radiates will come into you. I took this picture out of my bedroom window at the wonderful spiritual ecological community at Findhorn in the North of Scotland.

All the other pictures I took that night contained Archangel Gabriel's angels carrying divine feminine qualities. This extraordinary Orb of the Archangel himself will purify your mental and emotional energy as well as help you open to the wisdom of the divine feminine.

Archangel Gabriel is bringing a spirit to learn about enlightenment and Archangel Michael is protecting him. The Archangel's message is that it is time to open to enlightenment.

Picture 30

Photograph by Diana Cooper

Please sit quietly and absorb the light he radiates.

Archangel Gabriel is currently helping groups and individuals. We were sent a delightful picture of a young man with an Archangel Gabriel Orb on his arm. In that particular picture there were also fairies enjoying playing in the youth's energy but also absorbing the light of the archangel. The beings of light had all arrived to help him go through a transition in his life joyfully. This Orb is very helpful for youngsters who are moving into their teens and adulthood.

Archangels Gabriel and Michael are often seen merged together. In one picture we were sent of a group of teenagers dancing happily, a huge blue and white Orb was over one of the youngsters, bringing spirits of her loved ones to watch. It filled us with an understanding of how very much the angels and Archangels do to facilitate joy and togetherness.

Those in spirit are enriched by the knowledge that the young woman is well and, at unconscious level, the person still in a physical body feels their love and closeness.

Purification

The higher spiritual beings all work together for the highest good of all. They co-operate constantly. Sometimes they merge their energies to create a stronger force as you can see in picture (31), which is a close up of a wonderful green-turquoise Orb which was taken under Lizzie House's brother in law's coffee table. She says that there were more orbs in the bigger picture. They are bringing purification to this room and also to you, for everything is planned in the spirit world. None of these pictures have been taken by chance.

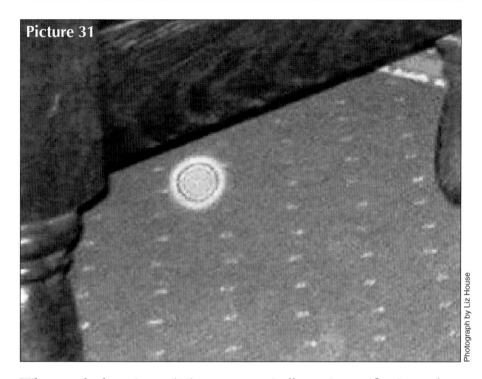

Picture 31

Photograph by Liz House

When you look at picture (31) you automatically receive purification and healing

In this Orb (31) Archangels Gabriel and Raphael have merged to bring purification and healing.

Many people are seeking their life purpose. Some are stumbling round feeling there must be a reason to be here on Earth. Others are actively searching. A great many have spiritual readings or astrological charts prepared to give them clues about what they are supposed to be doing.

But there is another way. You can sit quietly each day and ask Archangel Gabriel to bring you clarity about your life purpose and any other decision that is challenging you. When you are ready he will show you.

Chapter Fifteen

Archangel Uriel

Archangel Uriel is in charge of the angels of peace and is working to bring about peace on Earth by soothing conflict and promoting brotherhood and sisterhood. He looks after and helps to develop the solar plexus chakra, which governs your levels of confidence and self worth.

Humans tend to whirl their problems round and round in their minds. However, your mind is intimately connected to your solar plexus, which stores your fears and reacts to them. At a third dimensional level this centre is yellow. It is not by chance that libraries are traditionally painted yellow to soothe the mind so that people can concentrate and study. Yellow quietens the thoughts.

When you have an anxious or fearful thought it tightens up your solar plexus and affects your digestion and ability to assimilate or even truly consider new ideas. By calling on Archangel Uriel you can receive help to break the mental patterns and emotional chains that keep you stuck.

Most people still have yellow in their solar plexus so they are constantly picking up other people's fears. As you develop this chakra spiritually you regain your deepest wisdom and this centre transforms to gold. Then you can spread serenity and peace in a way that dissolves the fears of others. Without even knowing you are doing it you spread oil on troubled waters and truly become a peace maker.

Archangel Uriel's Orb is distinctive because it is a yellow gold colour, sometimes with tinges of purple or brown and it has an unusual texture and pattern which is very recognisable. His twin flame is Archangel Aurora, who helps with beginnings. She represents the dawn of the new and will assist you with any projects or starting again after a transition or life changing decision.

We were sent a picture of two children totally surrounded by angels of Archangel Uriel. They were yellow Orbs actually communicating with the youngsters, who were of course completely oblivious of them! Clearly Archangel Uriel was radiating confidence and peace to them and helping them to feel comfortable in the heavy surroundings of Earth.

You can ask Archangel Uriel to help you find self worth and ability to cope with your life's challenges with confidence. If you think about him during the day and ask in your prayers at night to go to his retreat in the etheric, you may receive direct teaching from him which will help you. And if you need assistance with something new, it is very important to request this assistance.

Remember to ask Archangel Uriel to help your children or any children you know, so that they can walk through life with their heads held high and a good feeling inside them.

Picture (32) is an Orb of Archangel Uriel himself. It contains peace and wisdom, so that you can absorb confidence, self worth and receive assistance with new beginnings. Where the chambers are open you can see Source light shining through and this can help you make a direct connection.

When you look at the Orbs in picture (32) you receive mental release, a sense of peace, an increase in confidence and help with new beginnings

In picture (32) you will see Archangel Uriel himself. I was on holiday in Thailand, standing on the veranda of my hotel in a tropical downpour. As I took photographs Orbs poured past. This Orb is one of them and I was buzzing with excitement when the golden ball showed on the screen. It transpired that many angels were urgently travelling to Bangkok where many animals were afraid of the storm. They were to calm and protect them.

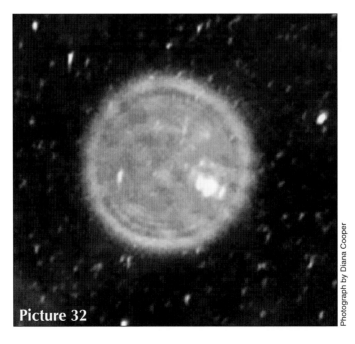

Picture 32

Photograph by Diana Cooper

In this picture you can see that some of the chambers within the Orb are active and are shining light into the area. When you look at this it will open you as much as possible to the level of light with which you can cope. The inactive cells of the Orb are preparing to gather negative energy, which they transmute to positive and beautiful light and radiate it out to those who need it. The light triggers your own wisdom, so that your level of confidence rises.

Exploring this Orb will help you to release old mental patterns and bring back the wisdom you have accumulated over your past lives in this planet or any other. It will also shower you with happiness. Try looking at it at the new moon, especially if you are contemplating a new step or venture towards your future. See also an exercise in the section of meditations and exercises with the Orbs to raise your consciousness.

Chapter Sixteen

Archangel Chamuel

Archangel Chamuel is the angel of love and he is charged with the mighty task of keeping the sparks of light in the hearts of humanity alight where they are almost extinguished. He also expands the flame of love in hearts that are open. He enables people to develop compassion, empathy, caring, understanding, co-operation, generosity and love.

He helps to bring lovers together, soothes difficult situations world wide and helps you see the best in others. Where someone is grief stricken one of his angels of love will arrive to soothe and hold you. He will help to heal broken hearts. You can recognise Archangel Chamuel's presence because his Orbs are the most beautiful soft pink and they have the ability to soften and heal your heart.

Chamuel's twin flame is Charity and the natural consequence of an open heart is generous giving to those less fortunate. Chamuel expresses the masculine aspect of love and Charity the feminine.

As with all archangels you can ask to visit his etheric retreat during your sleep to be enfolded and filled with love. An open heart attracts not only good relationships but all manner of abundance and happiness into your life.

We were sent the most beautiful photograph of a bride and groom on their wedding day. As they kissed, a huge pink Orb appeared behind the bride's heart. It was heart melting to see it.

We have often seen pink Orbs near couples in love, keeping their hearts open, so that they continue to see the divine in each other.

When you look at this picture (33) you open to love and a connection with the cosmic heart

Picture number (33) from Kari Palmgren in Norway is the most amazing picture of Archangel Chamuel with an angel of love. The Orb peeping out behind is Archangels Chamuel and Jophiel. Explore this in order to open your heart with love. It will help you dissolve all the old pain, especially the deeper layers which are pushed right down.

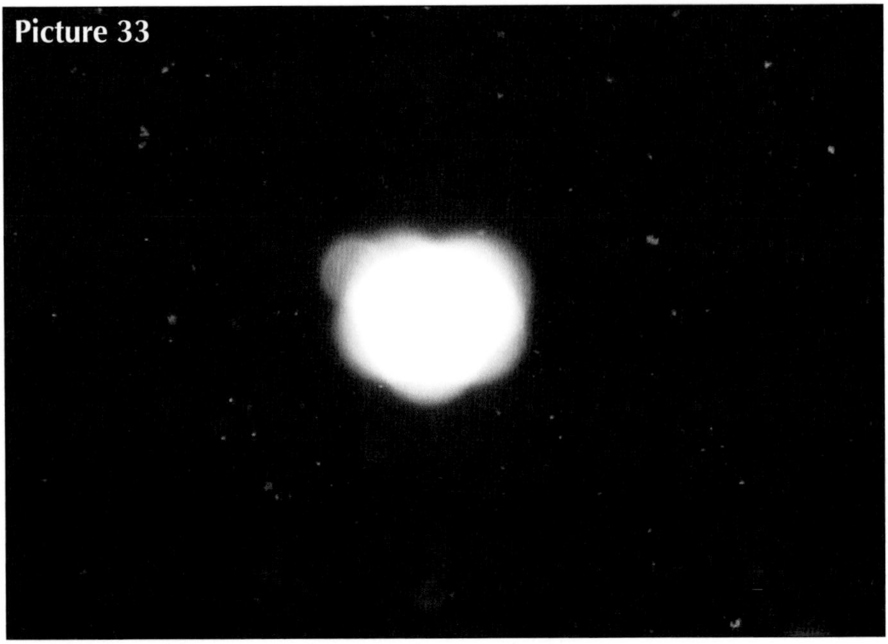

Picture 33

Photograph by Kari Palmgren

Your heart chakra is connected to the cosmic heart and through this picture you can also connect to the cosmic heart and listen to the heart beat of the universe.

We found it fascinating that this picture transpired to be 33 which number is the vibration of Christ consciousness; total unconditional love.

Chapter Seventeen

Archangels Sandalphon and Metatron

Archangel Metatron

Archangel Metatron is very connected with Egypt and his presence is often seen there. He works with the Lords of Karma, supervises the karmic records in the Hall of Records and is in charge of the recording angels.

After the fall of Atlantis he oversaw the building of the Great Pyramid, where the cosmic records are etherically kept. The Great Pyramid is, amongst other things, an intergalactic portal and antennae into the universe from Earth. Archangel Metatron still energises it and helps to keep the connections through it to other planets clear. We have been sent many photographs of spirit and angel Orbs which have been taken here.

Archangel Metatron is also in charge of the development of the Stellar Gateway chakra through which people connect with Source. During the times of Golden Atlantis the people had twelve chakras active and open, which meant they were able to access Source at all times. However when the energy devolved, five chakras closed down and this connection was no longer available to humanity. Now, at last, the opportunity to open our transpersonal chakras is once again being made possible. The task of awakening them is the journey to Source.

The twelve chakras are:

The Stellar Gateway – in the charge of Archangels Metatron and the Seraphim Seraphina.
The soul star – in the charge of Archangels Zadkiel and Mariel.
The causal – in the charge of Archangel Christiel.
The crown – in the charge of Archangel Jophiel.
The third eye – in the charge of Archangel Raphael.
The throat chakra – in the charge of Archangel Michael.
The heart chakra – in the charge of Archangel Chamuel.
The solar plexus – in the charge of Archangel Uriel.
The navel chakra – in the charge of Archangel Gabriel.

The sexual or sacral chakra – in the charge of Archangel Gabriel.
The base chakra – in the charge of Archangel Gabriel.
The Earth Star – in the charge of Archangels Sandalphon and Roquiel.

The Stellar Gateway chakra is a pure golden ball of energy, like a chalice which opens to receive light from Source. The transpersonal chakras, the Stellar Gateway, soul star and causal, above the crown cannot be opened in isolation. They must work in alignment with the Earth Star chakra which is below the feet.

More people are now accessing their Stellar Gateway, and we were sent an awesome picture (34) by Radka Jurcgova in which Archangel Metatron is helping her to access this chakra. The Orb above her head is of Archangels Gabriel and Metatron merged with an angel of protection. Her guardian angel is also by her shoulder as she prays.

Interestingly Kathy received an insight into the reason for the presence of the angel of protection in her Stellar Gateway. Kathy was accessing the Orb to enter the realms beyond but was told that she was not allowed to listen to Radka's prayers. Naturally Kathy would have honoured this anyway but it is fascinating to be told why the protective angel was there with Archangels Metatron and Gabriel. We were also interested to learn that the vibration of the prayers we make remain in our chakras.

As you look at this picture Archangel Metatron is helping you to access your Stellar Gateway.

When you look at the Orb in picture (34) you receive an invitation to the journey to access your stellar gateway

I had a wonderful experience, which I believe was a gift from Orb (34) which I often picture. I was walking through my local woods, bringing in my twelve chakras and working with them. It had long puzzled me why my soul star chakra, which holds our own and our ancestors', crystallised negative thought forms, often contained sludge. I reckoned I had done enough clearing on the energy from the genetic, ancestral and past life lines which often block this chakra!

So, as I strolled I asked about this and was reminded that I had frequently told the universe that I would accept and clear other people's 'stuff' so that the planet could ascend more quickly, and it is true, I often did make this offering. I had not realised it would affect my soul star so much. I asked if this was still the highest offering I could make and was clearly told 'No!' so I decided to rescind the offer!

Continuing to walk down the leafy path, I put up a blockage to anyone downloading through my soul star. Then I cleansed it. Immediately an awesome thing happened. I saw two balls of light, each about 2ft 6ins or 75cms diameter, one

Picture 34

Photograph by Radka Jurcgova

magenta and the other gold. They were radiating brightly above me in my soul star and Stellar Gateway. Soon after this Kumeka told me I had gone through another level of initiation.

Archangel Sandalphon

Archangel Sandalphon is the twin flame of Archangel Metatron. He is known as the tall angel because he gathers prayers from the angels and takes them to Source, so he links heaven and Earth. The name Sandalphon means one who wears sandals before the Almighty. Archangel Sandalphon is the patron saint of music.

He looks after the Earth Star chakras of everyone, which are below your feet. They are black and white, holding your divine potential.

When the energy from Source is accessed it flows down through all your chakras and into your Earth Star. Then it can flow along the ley lines to the Pyramids. When enough people open their twelve chakras and allow Source energy to flow through them this will re-energise the Pyramids and renew their power, so that our planet can take its proper place in the universe once more.

When the Earth Star is functioning properly the divine energy will be able to go directly into the earth and at last Mother Earth will be able to heal herself of all we have done to her. Also for the first time since Atlantis humans will be able to heal themselves totally.

Chapter Eighteen

Archangels Purlimiek, Gersisa and Butyalil

These three archangels have recently been assigned to work with our planet.

Archangel Purlimiek

This archangel is in charge of the nature kingdom and we have seen his Orb in several photographs, often surrounded by elementals and sometimes working with unicorns. Amongst other duties his angels are often placed in charge of big groups of fairies to help them evolve.

Archangel Gersisa

Archangel Gersisa works with Archangels Sandalphon and Roquiel, who are in charge of the Earth Star chakras of humanity.

She clears the energy round these centres whether they are awake or not, so that the light can come from Source through the person and enter the earth.

Archangel Gersisa is helping to bring about balance on the planet and the healing of the centre of it. In order to do this she is holding the Lemurian wisdom steady in the Earth. She is also working with beings of the Hollow Earth to keep the ancient energy awake and alive.

If you live in an area where the earth meridians are blocked this will affect your kundalini by blocking your energy flow. Your kundalini is the divine energy which flows through your spine. When fully awakened it travels up your spine to the crown and opens you to enlightenment.

It is sometimes depicted as a slumbering serpent and spiritual traditions aim to waken it slowly at a rate the individual can manage.

Archangel Gersisa is helping to keep all the ley lines clear, especially the ones deep in the centre of our planet. The impact of what she does affects the flow of the meridians in the Earth and also in people. People with ME are sensitives who have blocked meridians, so she can assist such individuals by helping to clear the earth ones.

Archangel Butyalil

In the cosmos there are huge currents of energy which affect our planet. Archangel Butyalil is in charge of keeping these in some sort of balance and synergy and, if he did not do this, Earth would be overwhelmed. So he works with Archangel Purlimiek of the nature kingdoms and Archangel Gersisa of the earth kingdoms to bring balance and harmony everywhere.

Archangel Butyalil works only with Earth so he has to link with other Archangels who are in charge of other planets. We asked if he was a cosmic diplomat but were gently reminded that he does not need to be as all the higher spiritual beings are working together for the highest good.

Archangel Butyalil works with the unicorns and their pure energy is helping him as they prepare the planet for its ascension. Now that the unicorns are helping humanity to progress it makes Archangel Butyalil's job easier. They are pleased that humans are waking up very quickly.

In the section about elementals in the glossary we talk about the new ones who are coming to the planet to help us. It was Archangels Purlimiek and Butyalil together who recently invited the esaks of earth, kyhils of water as well as other cleansers into the planet to clear and purify the energy. They also welcomed in new elementals to observe how we operate here.

Archangel Metatron is also working with Archangel Butyalil to make the conditions right for people to take the journey to open their Stellar Gateway chakras.

Clearing our psychic rubbish

Most of us have no concept of the impact of the energy we leave lying around. Parties where drugs and alcohol are consumed to excess attract negative energies and the entities who feed off them. Where these are outdoors, the revellers depart leaving nature to clear up after them. It is the psychic equivalent to discarding litter everywhere.

I tell the story in *Angel Answers* of a friend who visited a beauty spot which was strewn with bottles, cans and paper. She was disgusted. Suddenly a voice said in her head, 'And what about the psychic litter you are leaving here with your judgement!'

Groups where everyone sits round moaning about their fate or sharing their horrible problems produce a similar psychic fall out. It would be helpful if they called on Archangels Zadkiel or Gabriel to purify the negative energy released and then focus on their wholeness.

When you look at picture (35) you will receive a feeling of how important it is to look after nature

We include a picture of Archangel Purlimiek himself with a unicorn, carrying several spirits. He is the archangel of nature and this photograph was sent to us by

Picture 35

Photograph by Bernadette Gallagher

Bernadette Gallagher when she was walking in England's Peak District, right in the heart of nature, with her friend.

She took a whole series of photos of different shapes of trees, caves and rock formations which took on the forms of all different shapes and faces. Indeed, in other photographs she sent us we could see the nature spirits and elementals quite clearly.

When she wrote to us she described it as a magical day. She was clearly tuned into the wonderful energy and was blessed to receive a visit from Archangel Purlimiek.

When you look at picture (36) you receive a push to aspire to something better

Picture (36) was one of those taken by Kathy at Knowlton Church, where Kumeka often enters the planet. It is Kumeka with an angel of love and my higher self.

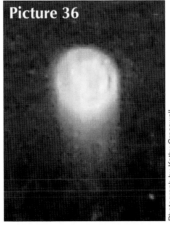

Picture 36

Photograph by Kathy Crosswell

Clearly he had brought this higher aspect of me to connect more closely with me but it also helps you to merge with your Higher Self. At the same time it increases your aspiration to help the world in some way.

Chapter Nineteen

Unicorns

Unicorns are seventh dimensional ascended white horses and fully of the angelic realms. In the Golden Times of Atlantis the people were all connected with their unicorns whose purity held them steady in the light. They withdrew from Earth when the energy of Atlantis devolved and now at last they are returning because enough people have raised their consciousness.

Unicorns look after children and those who are pure and innocent. They also work with those who have aspirations to help others and the world. So if you have a vision they will support you and give you the strength, dignity, faith and charisma you need to carry it through. They will enable you to deal with your challenges. They approach you when you are ready to serve and your light is clear and steady.

These great ones have spiralling horns which radiate from their third eyes in the middle of the forehead. Really these are emanations of enlightenment pouring from the third eye. If they direct this towards you, something deep within you changes.

They spread healing, purification and enlightenment to people and areas. Because their light is so bright their energy would fry you if they came too close, so they have to step their frequency right down. If you see a unicorn in the distance it looks like a very bright star. As it comes nearer to you and starts to lower its vibration so that you can accept it, it becomes bigger and paler. Even then some unicorn Orbs near children or even adults are very tiny. It will only ever approach you with as much energy as you can handle. Unicorns grant wishes especially those things that really benefit your soul. So ask for that which gives you soul satisfaction.

Clarify your vision

When you look at picture no (37) you will receive energy to help clarify your vision

When you look at Orb no (37) of Chris Saloschin, you will see his unicorn on his crown bringing him enlightenment and peace and helping him hold his vision. You can clearly see the translucence of its Orb. The crown is the centre

Picture 37

Photograph by Chris and Joy Saloschin

of enlightenment and wisdom, which opens to allow people to connect to the transcendent chakras above it.

When you have a burning desire to help people or to make something happen to benefit others, unicorns will see this light and come to you. We are seeing more and more pictures of people with little unicorn Orbs on their crowns but they are rarely as clear as the one above.

We have also seen unicorn Orbs in people's throat chakras. They are there to support the person in speaking out with clarity and dignity and to help clear the throat chakra. This awakens you to higher energies. So if you want to serve humanity in some way, even if it is something for your local community, and are nervous of speaking out, call in the unicorns and ask for help.

When you look at picture no (38) you will receive a knowing of innocence and joy

While we were writing the first edition of this book Kathy went to see her nephew's newborn baby daughter, called Summer. She was born in Christmas week. We smiled for there is such a lot of warmth and optimism in that name for a winter baby.

Unicorns love babies and children and so we were absolutely thrilled when Kathy took a photograph and there on the baby was a small unicorn Orb and, of course, her guardian angel.

Picture 38

Photograph by Jeni Floyd

The picture gave a message about the importance of the relationship between fathers and their children and how the angels and unicorns are helping them to bond. However, the quality of the picture was not clear enough and we have chosen another photograph with the same message.

Jeni Floyd sent us a fabulous picture no (38). Above the father and son is an angel of Archangel Gabriel bringing clarity to the father about the joys of parenthood. Any parent, particularly fathers, looking at this Orb will be opened up to a higher relationship with their children.

Chapter Twenty

Receive Energy from the Universe

I feel it is worth restating that Kumeka asked us to call this book *Enlightenment through Orbs* because you can be given messages and receive enlightenment simply by looking at them.

The pictures retain the light of the angelic beings and this contains spiritual information and knowledge. This means that through the Orb photographs you receive energy directly from the angels, archangels, unicorns and others of the spiritual hierarchy.

It will enter your consciousness whether you are open to it or not and start to prepare you for greater enlightenment. If you are already aware and consciously ready to receive the energy, it really can affect you at a deep level.

We find it amazing and awesome that the higher realms have found such a beautiful way to awaken and help us. These Orb pictures are a gift from the spiritual hierarchy so we hope you will accept them with the grace and love with which they are offered.

This is the first book in the series. *Ascension Through Orbs* is the second and we are guided to write *Healing Through Orbs* next. We offer these books with our love and blessings.

When you look at picture (39) you receive a whoosh of energy to awaken your heart centre

Photograph (39) was taken by Rosemary Stephenson and is a beautiful picture of tranquillity and harmony. It reminds you it is time to awaken your heart to joy and love. Peace and joy radiate from the page and the angels are helping to bring this about. However, there is much more.

When you look at this photograph you can see two Orbs in the light of the sun. These are angels who are using the energy of the sun to bring healing and peace to the area. In doing this they are generating an awakening of the heart chakras of everyone there. As humans, most of us are very good at burying or denying all our hurts, grief, rejections, feelings of inadequacy and disappointments.

Picture 39

Photograph by Rosemary Stephenson

In technological societies people are taught to think rather than to feel, so we tend to push the feelings into the back of our heart centres. If the emotions are

Picture 40

Photograph by Erica and Brian Thomas

never acknowledged or healed they may eventually cause a physical problem with the heart, lungs or back.

With this photograph the angels are offering an opportunity for awakening your heart centre and healing it.

When you look at picture (40) you will release fear of the unknown

So many people are sensitive to energy and have a slightly anxious feeling about their future or life in general. Many have a fear of travelling. In addition many individuals are nervous of the unknown without knowing why. Anyone who senses atmospheres will be affected by invisible energies.

Picture (40) was taken by Erica Thomas' husband, Brian, on 28th December 2007 at Pickering on the North Yorkshire Moors Railway.

These are all angels of Archangel Gabriel and guardian angels protecting the train and its passengers. Looking at this picture gives you a feeling of safety and security which releases fear of the unknown.

Meditations with the Orbs and exercises to raise your Consciousness – presented by Kathy Crosswell

Wywyvsil has provided a short insight into the emotions and feelings contained within some of the pictures. He asked Kathy to link with him and the angels and to share her very personal channelled experiences with you. He has also given meditations for your enjoyment and enlightenment.

The meditations are to help you attune to the message relating to each picture. Diana has given the exercises for each Orb.

Each time you meditate you will receive more light to raise your consciousness to a higher vibration. (Not all the channelled meditations have been included within this book. They are available at www.kathycrosssswell.com or www.healingorbs.com)

I know and appreciate that some people struggle to achieve a deep meditative state, but we don't actually think that matters too much. Your intentions and energy are still aligned with your angels. The following paragraphs contain some thoughts which you may find useful.

Meditations are personal to each and every one of us. There is no right or wrong way to meditate. If you are wondering how to start we would suggest you give yourself enough time. This can be anything from five minutes to a couple of hours. Choose a quiet space, a place to be comfortable, and ensure you are warm enough. Many people have great expectations and therefore put themselves under pressure and eventually give up. If this happens to you, it doesn't matter. You are obviously not meant to meditate at this time.

Some days you may try to meditate but fall asleep instead – obviously the angels need you to sleep at that time. Sometimes, your mind may keep bringing you back to tasks you need to do. Again, don't try and force yourself, either leave it or try again later.

You may find it beneficial to write a list of tasks to do and ask for help to achieve them. Leave the list to one side confident the tasks will be easy to complete. You will often find this brings you to the 'right space' and energy to enjoy your meditation.

As you start to take your journey you may find you are not following the words but are taken on a different path. Don't worry, just go with the flow. Obviously, the angels feel this new experience of discovery is much more important and relevant for you for that moment, so you can see meditations are for you and there is NO pressure – when it is right, it will just happen.

The following snippets into the essence of the pictures and the meditations are given with love from Wywyvsil and the angels. I hope you enjoy the Orbs as much as we do. If you wish to you can focus on the photograph, or you may prefer to look at the picture then close your eyes to meditate.

Picture 1 (Chapter 2) Receive courage to speak wisely and hear with understanding

Meditation – Getting to know your guardian angel

You find yourself walking round a lake. There are birds singing and ducks contentedly going about their business. They often stop to preen themselves and occasionally a fish breaks the water's surface to catch an insect which has landed on the lake. It is idyllic.

A little way ahead is a bench under a tree and you make your way to it and sit down. There you close your eyes and breathe in the atmosphere. With each in breath you feel your energy growing and this expands your aura, and you begin to sense another presence.

You open your eyes, but there is no one there. You shut them again but the feeling persists. It is a lovely sensation making you want to see who it is. You turn to face this other being and you are consumed with love, radiance, protection and joy.

You realise it is taking a shape and soon you are looking at your guardian angel. You are suddenly surprised as you are offered a gift. You ask about it. Once you have finished talking you drift into a hazy state. You are so happy. Slowly you become aware of birds twittering, the sun on your face and you realise you are sitting in your comfortable place.

Exercise to speak wisely and to hear with understanding

This is an exercise most of us need to practise. It can help your relationships and change your life.

1. Look at picture (1) for a few moments.
2. Light a candle and dedicate it to wise communication and understanding. If you have a particular circumstance in mind, ask for help with that.
3. Sit quietly and focus on your throat chakra. Breathe love into and peace out of it.

4. Visualise yourself with a huge blue aura.

5. Imagine a circumstance in which you need to speak wisely and to hear with understanding.

6. Picture your guardian angel speaking through you with immense wisdom and detachment.

7. Imagine the response and really listen to the underlying message. Then ask your guardian angel to help you understand their feelings.

8. Ask your angel to help you maintain this wisdom when you speak to this person or these people.

9. Thank your angel.

Picture 2 (Chapter 2) Receive joy and life force as well as purification and an opening of the consciousness to new opportunities.

This is the experience Kathy's guide, Wywyvsil gave her when she entered this Orb.

As I look into this Orb, I begin to sense every drop of water from the waterfall. It offers complete humility. It tastes so pure and clear it is extraordinary. It highlights all my impurities. I know I must drink of this water to cleanse and re-energise my being. I feel from my solar plexus the energy of this water and purity pushing into every cell of my body. It moves through one to the next and to the next. It feels so fresh and each cell tingles with the newness of its energy. Immediately a sensation of complete unselfish love, kindness and excitement runs through my chakras.

I am so humbled, I want to cry. This Orb has collected the Earth's energy and given it to me! I am so privileged and grateful. It reminds me just how much I love life and this planet.

Meditation – Feel pure and at one with the Earth's life force

You find yourself sitting by a waterfall. You are warmed by the sunlight and cooled by the gentle breeze. On the wind you can hear birdsong, which makes you smile. You smell fragrant flowers near by and this makes you smile even more. As you are sitting there you reflect on how wonderful nature is. Without knowing it you begin to realise that the sound of the water falling has heightened your senses.

Its repetition draws you in and you begin to breathe in rhythm with the falling water, making you more relaxed. You wish you could stay in this moment for ever. You notice you are being covered in spray and it is cold and refreshing.

You close your eyes to enhance this sensation. This allows you to enjoy every drop of spray which lands on your body. You open your eyes and to your amazement you are now within one of these drops of water. You can see out, but you know you are enclosed and it feels great!

You can hear the Earth's rhythm. It is like a heart beat and your body begins to resonate with the pulse of the Earth. The energy in your body intensifies to the point where you lose sight of your physical self. You are at one with the water drop. You are clean, pure, fully energised and know that purification is running through the very essence of you.

You begin to recognise the Earth's remedies being given to you and you welcome these. You allow this to continue for as long as is necessary. When you are fulfilled you drop into the cascade of churning water at the base of the waterfall.

The noise is awesome and the power beyond any force you have experienced before, taking you to a higher vibration and another level of cleansing given by the sound. Your chakras have been re-aligned with the Earth and all she has to offer. 'Amazing' cannot even begin to describe how you feel. As the water quietens you find yourself back in your physical frame, re-energised and at peace.

You close your eyes and when you open them you notice you are in your comfortable place bursting with happiness.

Exercise to receive joy and life force as well as purification and an opening of the consciousness to new opportunities

1. Look at picture (2).
2. If you possibly can, go to a physical place of high energy, the sea, a lake or waterfall, a mountain, a beauty spot or somewhere in nature that feels really energising to you.
3. If you cannot visit it in person find a picture or photograph of such a place.
4. Call in the angels.
5. Ask them to collect joy and life force from this place and bring it back to you.
6. Sense the energy being brought to you. Feel it purifying you. Then breathe in the joy and life force.
7. Imagine your mind opening to new opportunities.
8. Ask the angels to bring these to you.
9. Thank the angels for their work on your behalf.
10. Keep breathing in that higher consciousness and be open to the new opportunities.

Picture 3 (Chapter 3) Receive energy to work with angels to help your child

This is the experience Kathy's guide, Wywyvsil gave her when she entered this Orb.

As I look into the Orb the bright blue hue draws me in. I am safe and very relaxed. I am reassured that I no longer have to tackle everything on my own. The burden of accountability and responsibility has been removed from me. I feel as if I am in a big cuddle, like being protected when my father used to hug me as a child.

Immediately there is a sense of 'being in the moment', in a wholeness which is just there for me. I know without a doubt that I will guide my children with confidence and happiness. If this Orb could smile it would, as it is immensely proud of these children. It is protecting them at a soul level.

It is bringing happiness and the approval to try. It doesn't matter if you don't succeed, or if you succeed. It doesn't judge. It is bringing to the children the knowledge of how to go about things in the best way. It wishes others to enjoy and respect each of these children as they grow physically, emotionally and spiritually. The Orb itself has a depth beyond comprehension and it brings protection from Source itself. When you are enclosed by this Orb you cannot see out.

Visualisation to keep your child safe

When you ask a spiritual being to do something, you can assist them by visualising it being accomplished.

1. Look at picture (3).
2. Light a candle.
3. Picture your child safe, happy and well.
4. Ask their guardian angel to enfold them in their wings and imagine this happening.
5. Ask Archangel Michael with his sword and shield to stand by your child and protect them. Picture this as clearly as you can.
6. Ask Archangel Uriel to give your child confidence and a sense of peace. Then imagine a golden light enveloping them.
7. Now do whatever you need to and do not worry about them. Let the angels look after them knowing that they will be totally protected.
8. Please note that once you have placed angelic protection round your loved one, your prayers and visualisations have conferred extra safety on them.

Picture 4 (Chapter 4) Receive the message that angels support your decisions

Meditation – Serenity is achievable

You find yourself in a room full of people. Everyone is talking, yet you are very alone. The world is standing still, whilst everything continues around you. You wonder why you are at this event. Gradually, however, you begin to feel different, no longer alone. In fact it is as if you have been consumed by a calm and peaceful energy.

You look around and notice how each person in the room is behaving. With each realisation you become more and more at peace, you begin to feel happy and you can't help but smile.

Your energy is now radiating out to everyone, inviting them to talk to you and you are pleased for this to happen. You can't believe how good this feels. You see that people are smiling and coming towards you. They are keen to enjoy your energy and company as much as you are enjoying it.

Very soon you are talking to many people and the atmosphere has lifted, bringing a sense of serenity and peace to the room. You are now starting to laugh and this is infectious. Those around you laugh too, bringing more and more people into your energy. By now the event is just perfect. You know that whatever you do you are guided and supported and this feels great! With this realisation you find yourself back in your comfortable place refreshed and enlightened.

Ask angels to support your decisions

1. Look at picture (4).
2. Sit down quietly and tell the angels of your decision, whatever it is.
3. Ask them to support it.
4. Know that, no matter what, your angels are helping you to do what you have chosen.
5. Move forward with confidence.

Picture 5 (Chapter 5) Receive protection from electrical appliances

This is the experience Kathy's guide, Wywyvsil gave her when she entered this Orb.

As I look at this picture I feel the low vibrations from the television. The sensations are felt in my heart, third eye and throat chakras. They feel heavy, sluggish and my shoulders and back have started to ache. The crystals within this picture want to breathe, but they struggle with the lack of opportunity to do so. The Orb enfolds me and I feel its sticky texture.

This allows it to vibrate at a frequency low enough to 'catch' the negative vibrations being transmitted by the programme on the television. It transmutes the energy and uses it to reduce the charge in the ions surrounding this television. This Orb is the angel of the building, and like most others it has huge depth and many facets.

It has compartments which gather in damaging energies from the technology in the building. It also collects the negative intentions like those which emanate from so many of our TV and radio programmes, CDs and DVDs. It then transmutes this energy and brings the positive energy back for the 'greater good' of the house. Also within this Orb is a tall and gentle man who is quite proper in his ways.

Meditation – to understand the impact of electricity on our energies

You find yourself sitting in a very large warm cave lit by a fire. There are tools made of flint scattered everywhere. You get up and walk outside to see an amazing panoramic view.

The planet is lush and vibrant. You breathe in deeply. Your lungs are cool and clean. You blink your eyes and they feel awake and alert. You stretch and shake yourself from head to toe. You sense your energy running through all your chakras and into your expanded aura. It feels wonderful. As you turn to go back into the cave you realise it is very hot and stuffy.

Instead of the cave you are in an electrical shop. You breathe in deeply. Your lungs are tight and restricted. You open your eyes and they squint a little. They feel tired and strained. Your chakras and body are exhausted and they ache. You turn to leave the shop and find the door is closed.

As you open the door you are immediately showered by black tourmaline dust, which cleanses your aura and body from the electrical charges attached to you. You walk forward 'clean' again. This is great, just as you felt in the ancient times. With this thought you return to your comfortable place clean and refreshed.

Receive protection from electrical vibrations

1. Obtain a black tourmaline crystal. All crystal shops sell them.
2. Place it on picture (5) for half an hour.
3. Then put it in front of your television screen or any other electrical goods.
4. This will enable the angels to work with the energy of the crystal to protect you.

Picture 6 (Chapter 5) Receive a feeling of love and protection

This is the experience Kathy's guide, Wywyvsil gave her when she entered this Orb.

As I focus on just the Orb, it literally takes my breath away. Immediately I sense another being breathing with me. I am able to breathe symbiotically with the sprit within the Orb. It feels wonderful. It is quiet and like fluffy cotton wool. The spirit is gently wrapped in the 'cotton wool' and peaceful and content.

I know he is a male, and is focused on bringing his love to the family. He is determined to make sure the family knows he is here. His main concern is to raise the family's understanding of the negative impact television can have on their enlightenment. He genuinely wants what is best for his family and is making his presence known.

Meditation – awareness of suggestion

You believe yourself to be a 2D character in a cartoon script. You are running and you hurt yourself. This happens again and again. It doesn't matter to you because the cartoonist can simply repair you. You have no sense of being a drawn character so you give and receive physical and emotional trauma without thought.

The cartoonist decides to have your character carried into the sky by an oversized eagle with very long sharp talons. It drops you from a great height. You break many bones, but in the next scene you are on crutches and then by the scene after that you are back running around again. You begin to feel invincible.

You know that whatever is done to you or you do to others will not hurt you or anyone else. You decide to go outside to take a walk and cross a bridge over a flowing stream. Instead of walking on the path you climb onto the wall which protects passers by from falling into the stream. You now know you are invincible!

As you reach the centre, the highest point, you lose your footing and slip. You stop yourself from falling just in time. This shakes you. Slowly and humbly you step off the wall and onto the path. You feel very small and mortal all of a sudden, and you realise the cartoon had suggested you are invincible and you had believed this to be true. You sit down breathing heavily.

You lower your head to relax and as you do this you become aware of a presence near by. You look up and standing before you is a beautiful angel. You smile knowing that this angel has protected you and you offer him your thanks. You realise you have been helped to see how easy it is to be drawn into situations. You know that to avoid this you must draw on inspiration and follow your heart.

It is with this thought you return to your comfortable place enlightened.

Receive a feeling of love and protection

1. Look at picture (6).
2. Close your eyes and relax.
3. Think of someone you know who has passed over. They may even have died before you were born, such as a great grandparent to whom you are linked.

4. Ask Archangel Michael to bring their spirit to you.
5. Imagine his deep blue energy right round you enfolding you.
6. Sense the love this person has for you. Open your heart to receive it.
7. Send them love too. Thank them for coming and let them go.
8. Notice how you feel. Then open your eyes.

Picture 7 (Chapter 5) Receive a knowing that angels look after you when you are out in nature

Meditation – snakes and ladders

You find yourself draped from head to toe in thermal clothing. You have snow shoes on your feet with ice spikes. You are climbing a steep glacier, dotted with deep crevices. The sun is out and the shimmer blinding. The glacier looks glorious, sharing its pale blue almost transparent hue.

You are alone but you know you are completely guided by your angels. You wear a rope harness which you attach every step of the way. You have been climbing now for three hours and you are becoming a little tired. In truth you are complacent. You are not 'in tune' with your guides as well as you were earlier in the day. You attach your rope ready for your next ascent.

Then you step on ice which breaks under your weight and fall a long way into the ravine. You stop suddenly as your rope reaches its limit and find yourself dangling in your harness. You cannot see the bottom of the ravine. You realise you should have stopped to rest and set up camp for the night, but you ignored this 'knowing' and continued.

You don't panic. You just wonder what to do. Again you are faced with an all consuming knowing. You know you only have to swing yourself back and forth and you will reach a ledge. From it a path leads to the top of the ravine.

It is at this precise moment you realise that you are totally guided. You understand life can be like 'snakes and ladders', depending on whether you ignore your guided inspiration or listen and accept it. With this enlightened moment you find yourself back in your comfortable place.

Know that the angels are looking after you when you are out in nature

1. Look at picture (7).
2. Call in your guardian angel and Archangel Gabriel.
3. Go for a walk in the countryside or a park or beach.
4. As you walk be aware of the presence of your guides and protectors.
5. Try to sense where they are around you.
6. Notice how you feel being looked after.

7. You return from your walk thank them and know that your trust in them has brought them closer to you.

Picture 8 (Chapter 6) Receive a transmutation of fear to confidence

This is the experience Kathy's guide, Wywyvsil gave her when she entered this Orb.

When guardian angels come together, as in this picture, I get the feeling of a collective strong motherly protection. This is quite different from the gentleness I feel from a single one. I was given a glimpse of responsibility undertaken by them. They certainly are a force to be reckoned with. The guardian angels in this picture needed to protect these people and were pleased to tell me that they had done so.

Meditation – for confidence and clarity

You find yourself standing on a cliff looking out to sea. There is a chill in the air and you feel a storm brewing. You begin to notice the wind getting stronger. The ocean starts to swell and you hear the waves crashing against the rocks below you.

The wind is now blowing really hard and you brace your legs firmly, open your arms wide and tilt your head back. You feel amazingly empowered. It is at this moment you realise your guardian angel is standing with you and this makes you really happy. You push your chest out, take a deep breath and shout loudly into the wind "I am not afraid, I welcome your energy".

As you shout these words you are surrounded in light, which illuminates all around you. This raises your confidence to a point where you are at complete peace despite the storm raging strongly. You know that you have the strength and courage to meet any opportunity which comes your way.

With this understanding the storm starts to recede and the sun breaks through the clouds bathing you in light and love. This gives you warmth and clarity which brings you back to your comfortable place.

Angels help you transmute fear to confidence

1. Look at picture (8).
2. Focus on a fear you hold and name it aloud if possible. If you do not wish to vocalise it, think about it very clearly.
3. Say or think, 'I now invoke my guardian angel to help me transmute this fear and bring me confidence.'
4. Breathe into your solar plexus and picture a golden ball of light and wisdom filling it.
5. You can do this as often as you need to.

Picture 9 (Chapter 7) Receive from the universe a certainty that love is there for you

Meditation – to receive love

You find yourself walking aimlessly. You spot something in the distance and walk towards it. You find it is a moving staircase. You step onto it and are slowly carried upwards, through the clouds, until eventually you reach a door. It opens and you step inside. You are in a room with no doors or windows and the entrance you came through has disappeared. You walk around trying to find a way out of the room. You quickly realise there is no exit, so you sit quietly on the floor to consider what to do.

A note floats gently to the floor and you pick it up. It reads, "Are you ready to receive love?" Nothing happens, but you are beginning to consider the question. As your consciousness begins to accept the invitation an abundance of love, light enters the room and a warm feeling starts to grow inside you.

The more you accept the love, the more light shines on you. The room slowly dissolves. As this happens you find you are enveloped by an angel of love. You know now that you are ready to accept love abundance into your life. With this recognition you find yourself back in your comfortable place bathed in pure white angel love.

Invoke an angel of love

An invocation is a very powerful way of drawing the forces of the universe in to help you. Put your heart and soul into your request.

1. Look at picture (9).
2. Light a candle and dedicate it to love.
3. Say aloud or in your head, 'In the name of God I now invoke an angel of love to come to me.'
4. Trust that one has responded and is with you.
5. Pause and allow yourself to feel its light and love enfold you.
6. Let the love enter every cell of your body.
7. Knowing that you are totally loved and lovable, how differently do you feel? How lovingly can you respond to others?

Picture 10 (Chapter 7) Receive an understanding of the unconditional love of animals

As you look into this picture you can see the surprise on the little dog's face. You see surprise but no fear. This gorgeous animal is completely at peace with angels.

Exercise to feel the unconditional love of animals

1. Look at photograph (10).
2. Next time you are with an animal mentally call on an angel of love to enfold it and you.
3. If you can, physically stroke the animal. If you cannot touch it imagine that you are stroking it. What does it feel like? Can you smell it?
4. Feel your heart opening to receive all the love that this creature has.
5. Let the love fill you up from your head to your toes.
6. Thank it for loving you unconditionally.
7. Every time you see an animal send it your unconditional love.

Picture 11 (Chapter 8) Receive unconditional love for you and from those you love in spirit

Receive unconditional love for yourself and those you love from those in spirit

1. Look at picture (11).
2. Think of any friends and loved ones in spirit and imagine them smiling down on you and sending love. Open your heart and receive it.
3. Then remember all your ancestors in spirit, whether or not you knew them. Even if you did not feel loved by them when they were alive, they have now let go of their ego and their baggage that stopped them from caring.
4. Now that they are in the spirit world their consciousness has expanded. They are pouring love down on to you.
5. Know that you are loved for yourself. However good or bad, successful or unsuccessful, clever or lacking in intellect you are, they love you. They see your pains, struggles and disappointments and love you more than ever.
6. Put your hand on your heart and feel it opening to receive all this love that is there for you.
7. Send this love to your friends and family.

Picture 12 (Chapter 8) Receive a desire to connect with animals and the peace this brings

Meditation – harmony

You find yourself in the middle of a lake sitting on a raft, cross-legged and relaxed and your face is slightly tilted upwards towards the sun, which is gentle and warm. There is the occasional small wave which moves the raft a little, otherwise there is no movement.

As you are sitting there you sense the energy from the elements enter your being. The sun gives you vibrancy and energy, the gentle air on your face and skin is fresh and pure, the energy of the Earth brings serenity and nutrition and you feel the water renewing your energy and this feels brilliant.

You become aware that your breathing is different and it has taken on the rhythm of the lake. It is at one with the lake, the air, the sun and Earth. You are peaceful and in harmony with yourself and the elements.

As you are relaxing you rise from the water to be met by a beautiful dragon. He is blue grey in colour, smooth to the touch and magnificent. He drops his shoulder to invite you to climb on his back, which you do eagerly. He stands again and you can feel his powerful muscles getting ready to fly.

With that, he slowly and steadily begins to soar up into the sky. The force of the wind against your body is exhilarating and you just love flying with your dragon. Slowly, you notice that another dragon has joined you and together they soar as if they are the wind. They fly to a volcano where another dragon appears from the flames of its core.

It brings with it the energy of creation and together they fly to the centre of the Earth through the intricate caves and tunnels. All this time you are privileged to ride with these magnificent beings.

At the Earth's core is another dragon that has been waiting to join you. Together they fly you back to the raft. As you climb down onto the raft, you know you are surrounded in perfect harmony by the wonder of nature. The dragons bring to you the forces of earth, wind, fire and water. You are loved, protected and completely at one with nature and the dragons.

It is with this realisation that you know you have been enlightened to a purpose much greater than that known to you before. It is with this thought and the love and support of the dragons that you find yourself back in your comfortable place.

How to connect with animals and enjoy the peace this brings

1. Look at picture (12).
2. Find a place where you can be quiet and undisturbed.
3. Light a candle or a joss stick. Play quiet music if possible.
4. Close your eyes and breathe comfortably until you feel relaxed.
5. Visualise a unicorn approaching you. It is bright white and its horn is glowing with light.
6. It is bending and touching your heart with the tip of its horn. You may sense your heart expanding or glowing.
7. Your unicorn lies down beside you and you feel peaceful and safe.

8. Now animals are coming to you with peace in their hearts. There are all sorts from tigers to puppies. Greet them all. Look into their eyes and exchange peace and love.

9. When you have finished, thank all those who came to connect with you.

10. Thank your unicorn and receive a message from him. Then watch him stand up and walk away.

11. Open your eyes and notice how your heart feels.

Of course, it is even more effective to do steps 8 and 9 with physical animals.

Picture 13 (Chapter 8) Receive healing for your soul

Meditation – what is love?

You find yourself aged seven and sitting happily in a classroom. Your teacher asks, "What is love?" A child explains that it is when her daddy tells her he loves her. Another child says 'when my dog is pleased to see me' and your friend states it is when mummy cuddles me. The teacher responds warmly saying love sounds great.

She asks you to consider how you feel when you are giving your love to another person. You answer saying it makes you special, wanted, safe and it makes you happy. "I see," says the teacher, "so love is all about you, is that right?" You look at your friends who look back at you. You all look lost and unable to answer her.

Your teacher is a lovely lady, with a smiley face and she could see you were all a little confused. To help you really understand all about love she suggests a game. She asks the children with blond hair to stand on the right of the classroom and all the remaining children to sit at their desks.

The blond haired children are to play at being the mummies and daddies to the rest of the children in the class. You are a blond haired child. One of the brown haired children runs up to you and says, "Mummy, look at the picture I drew, isn't it good?" You answer, "Yes it is lovely."

But you weren't really interested and you looked a bit grumpy when you said it. The brown haired child walked away saddened by your response. Immediately, your heart starts to ache and you feel bad, because you can see you upset this child. You then realise that love is about giving as well as receiving.

You run over to the child and say 'I'm sorry, what I meant to say is your picture is brilliant and I love it!' In an instant the brown haired child smiles and she gives you a big hug. You could see your teacher smiling at you. She knew you had learnt what love is really all about. With this you find yourself in your comfortable place full of love and contentment.

Visualisation to receive healing for your soul

1. Find a place where you can be quiet and undisturbed.
2. Look at picture (13) then close your eyes and relax by focusing on love as you breathe in and peace as you breathe out.
3. Think of a quality that would satisfy your soul. It may be love, peace, job satisfaction, creativity, friendship, joy or service. Imagine your life with this quality.
4. Sense Archangel Michael surrounding you in a bright blue light, giving you strength and courage.
5. Feel Archangel Zadkiel's violet light entering the cells of your body transmuting anything that stops you finding your soul satisfaction.
6. Ask Archangel Raphael to shine his green healing energy into your being.
7. Relax into the feeling this brings you and trust that all things new are coming to you.
8. Thank the spiritual hierarchy for the help they are bringing you.

Picture 14 (Chapter 8) Receive a knowing that humans must expand their consciousness to honour animals

Exercise to help all humans expand their consciousness and honour animals

1. Look at picture (14).
2. Think of an animal, anything from a lion to a mouse, a horse to a monkey. If possible see a real, live animal.
3. Consider which planet and universe the animal comes from.
4. What could be their purpose in choosing to incarnate on Earth?
5. What are they learning here? What are they teaching?
6. What qualities are they developing?
7. What understandings are they taking back to their planet of origin?
8. If you could talk to it what would you like to communicate to this animal? Telepathically send your message.
9. Do you receive a reply? If you could hear it what would it be?
10. Thank the animal for its courage in coming to Earth and for its contribution to the diversity of life.
11. Notice if your feelings towards this animal have changed.

Picture 15 (Chapter 9) Receive joy and healing

This is the experience Kathy's guide, Wywyvsil gave her when she entered this Orb.

As I enter this Orb's energy, I begin to feel my body vibrate. I learn that there is a unique sound that resonates with every Orb. These vibrations are felt within the cells in our bodies and in return we resonate with all in nature. I am astounded that everything has its own resonation, intensity and pitch. I am told that the ability to bring health and abundance to others will come to those who can understand this energy and use this for the 'greater good'. Working with this Orb will begin that journey of discovery.

Exercise to receive joy and healing through sound

1. Look at picture (15)
2. Play, hum or listen to a beautiful piece of music or singing.
3. Call in Fekorm and ask him to help you receive joy and healing deep into your cells from the sound.
4. Feel the energy moving deep within you.

Picture 16 (Chapter 9) Receive protection and an understanding of the awesome power of sound

Meditation – to be healed by sound

You find yourself standing between two pillars. You place a hand and a foot against each one, tilt your head to the skies and close your eyes. As you do this a strong energy enters your body and the floor beneath you disappears. You trust completely knowing you will not fall. You look around and realise you are in a sphere.

It fills with golden light and a gentle sound can be heard. It is humming and it gets louder and louder. You become aware of every cell in your body. The golden light and the resonance of the sound enter your body. It begins to vibrate. You are aware of the healing affect this is having on you.

You notice there are impurities within you which are not resonating to the sound or the golden light. You let go and gently drift into the centre of a crystal singing bowl. Surrounding the singing bowl are many different sized gongs and also very tiny singing bowls. As you lie in the bowl you know some of your cells are still not vibrating at the right frequency. You settle in the bowl and focus on each cell which has impurities. You ask the angels to bring healing for your cells. Immediately, the most amazing sound begins to consume you.

It enters your very essence. You watch as every cell receives the healing it requires. This crescendo of sound happens seven times. Please take as long as you need to ensure all your cells receive this healing. Once your last cell has enjoyed its sound bath you realise that one by one the sounds begin to quieten. Finally, there is only the glorious sound of silence which remains. As you lie there your body enjoys the wonderful sensation of being energised and cleansed. Take a moment before returning to your comfortable place.

Exercise to enhance your protection and receive an understanding of the awesome power of sound

1. Look at picture (16).
2. Play a piece of powerful uplifting music.
3. Close your eyes and visualise the deep blue orb of Archangel Michael protecting you.
4. Picture Archangel Zadkiel placing a violet light over you to transmute any lower energy.
5. Ask Fekorm to help you accept and understand the awesome power of the sounds you are listening to.
6. Then relax and let the angels and the music do their work.

Picture 17 (Chapter 10) Receive permission from those in spirit to get on in life

Meditation – putting things right

You find yourself sitting on a large flat rock in the depth of a forest. In your hand is a note and it is blank. You are staring at it, not knowing what to do. You are troubled as you have run away following an argument with your parents.

Your attention moves from the note as you become aware of a beautiful white light through the trees. It is coming towards you. You are star struck by its beauty and watch with interest and anticipation. As it gets close you realise you are in the presence of a unicorn. It walks right up to you and bows its head for you to touch. You slowly raise your hand to stroke its nose. As you touch it you feel its mighty horn gently engage with your third eye.

At this moment you get a glimpse of your family at home frantic with worry. They are scared for you and are crying and shouting. They don't know what to do. The unicorn backs away slightly and looks at you with fixed eyes. He focuses on you and you can't control what you feel. Your heart wants to burst. You realise with complete certainty that you love your family so much. With that the unicorn breaks its gaze from you and wanders away slightly.

You become aware again of the note in your hand. It says 'I love me, I love me, and I forgive me.' You want to go home immediately to run into the arms of your family. The unicorn raises its head again and looks at you. Instantaneously a bright flash of light appears and surrounds you.

As the light recedes you find yourself standing by your front door. You are so excited. You open the door and run inside. Your family are so pleased to see you and you are over the moon to see them, life has never been better. You look for the note in your hand but instead there is a pure white feather. It is given to you with love. Smiling and happy, you embrace your family. You hold this feeling for a long time until you are ready to find yourself back in your comfortable place.

Receive permission from those in spirit to get on with life

The Orbs in photograph (17) will help anyone who has been bereaved to get on with their lives and enjoy each moment again. Remember that life is continuous for yourself and those in spirit. They are just a thought away and the angels bring them to see you. When you are stuck in grief you hold your loved ones, in spirit, back too.

1. Look at picture (17).
2. Close your eyes and relax.
3. Ask Archangel Gabriel to bring your loved ones to visit you. Feel the presence and the love that is coming to you.
4. See your loved ones in front of you.
5. Listen to them giving you permission to get on with your life.
6. Thank them for this and tell them you set them free too to continue their experiences in spirit. Know that their angels will still bring them to visit you.
7. Decide on one new thing that you will do.
8. Ask the unicorns to help you emerge from your cocoon and spread your wings.

Picture 18 (Chapter 10) Receive a direct unicorn connection

Receive a direct unicorn connection

1. Look at picture (18).
2. Close your eyes and breathe in the energy of the unicorn orb.
3. Visualise your unicorn coming to you, a beautiful white horse with a horn of light from his third eye.
4. Touch your unicorn and look into his eyes.
5. He has something important to tell you. Listen and communicate telepathically.
6. Thank him for coming to you.
7. Open your eyes and be aware of unicorn energy in your daily life.

Picture 19 (Chapter 10) Receive love and healing for yourself and a knowing that your loved ones are receiving it too.

Meditation – enjoy meeting your loved ones

You find yourself at a fairground. It is very busy with people queuing for rides and the atmosphere is electric. You are really excited. You walk through the crowds and you realise there is an attraction ahead of you which no one else seems to be aware of.

Being curious you walk over to it. It is a train, which rambles through beautiful surroundings. The attendant opens the door to let you step inside. There is a free seat next to you. It starts to move and you are taken through a garden filled with vibrant colourful and fragrant flowers. There is a small waterfall which glistens in the sunlight and also song birds singing in the garden.

The carriage comes to a halt and you notice for the first time that someone has climbed in next to you. As you turn round you find you are sitting next to someone you loved dearly, who is now in spirit. You can see this person clearly and hear every word they say. You are completely caught up in the moment. You are not aware the train has started to move again.

You travel through different scenes, but nothing distracts you from your conversation. When you have finished your carriage stops by a bench. You both get off and embrace.

Your loved one sits on the bench and tells you that any time you wish to have a chat all you have to do is ask. They are waiting and ready to meet you. Remembering your wonderful journey you find yourself back in your comfortable place, complete with the understanding that you can connect with your loved ones.

Receive love and healing for yourself and a knowing that your loved ones are receiving it too

Note that for this exercise your loved one does not have to be in spirit. They can also receive love and healing while in a physical body.

1. Look at picture (19)
2. Pick or buy some flowers, bless them and dedicate them to your loved one.
3. If your loved one has passed over you may like to visit their grave or create a corner of your garden or balcony for them. If you cannot do either of these things find a tree out in nature and mentally dedicate it to them. If you want to send love and healing to someone you love, who is still alive, in the same way dedicate a space for them.
4. Place the flowers in this place.
5. Stand here and think lovingly about your loved one.
6. Ask the angels to bring you love and healing. Breathe it in as it arrives in an orange ball.
7. Ask the angels to send them love and healing and picture them enfolded in it.
8. Thank the flowers, the angels and your loved ones.

Picture 20 (Chapter 10) Receive love, protection and enlightenment

Meditation – Nirvana

You find yourself travelling very quickly. You are bathed in a stream of golden light and feeling wonderful. You have no idea where you are going or how long it has taken. You become aware of a light so bright it dazzles you. As you reach it you realise you have come to the angelic council chamber which is full of angels.

As you stand before them, you are given an opportunity beyond your wildest dreams. You are told that for that day you have the responsibility of restoring harmony and peace to Earth. You are asked to observe all activity which takes place on Earth. You must then decide what you will do to make a difference. You are amazed, pleased and a little scared.

You are given a special sphere and as you look into it you can see Earth and all that is occurring there. You begin to notice the complexity that is Earth. As you observe, you are privileged to watch the angels at work and are amazed to see the number of Orbs that are about and why they are needed. You just can't take it all in. You begin to realise that the whole of the human race has to raise its consciousness to make any difference at all to the harmony of Earth.

You recognise the importance of people's connections with spirit and how easily this can be achieved and enhanced. However you are also aware just how far the human race has to go. You are eager to undertake your role today.

You ask the angels to go en masse to Earth and to focus on human consciousness. Then, as you observe their activity, you realise the angels are already doing this. The energy is transforming in people all the time. Sometimes it expands and changes colour and at other times it diminishes and is only just noticeable.

Many humans have no distinguishable light at all and this really touches you. It unsettles you a little as often negative emotions and behaviours impact on you. You ask the angels to focus on bringing positive energy to those people in darkness. You also ask them to give every person an opportunity to shine even more by becoming more enlightened. You sit back and watch the angels lighting up people. It again highlights your consciousness level as you see that some people shine whilst others do not.

You turn to the angelic council and ask for their support to keep your light bright and positive. They state that when you return to Earth you will be accompanied by a very special angel. You will be reminded daily of your role to raise the consciousness of those on Earth. This will bring about harmony and peace and reconnect Earth's ley lines to help the planet restore itself to its full magnificence.

With this in mind, you are aware of an angel surrounding you in light and unconditional love. Together you enter the golden ray which returns you gently back to your comfortable place. You spend time to reflect on this meditation and to sit for a while to get to know the angel.

Receive love, protection and enlightenment

1. Look at photograph (20) of the unicorn, angel of love and spirit of a loved one.
2. Ask the unicorn to transmute the old and stuckness within you.
3. Be aware of the spirit of a wise one near you.
4. Open yourself to receive love, protection and enlightenment.
5. Still your mind and listen to the message they are bringing you.
6. Know that you can hear divine guidance more clearly each time you do this.

Picture 21 (Chapter 11) Receive a feeling of empathy with the elementals

Meditation – join the elementals

You find yourself sitting near a beautiful pond with flowers in full bloom. Fish are darting between the reeds and frogs are popping up occasionally to get some air. You enjoy watching these goings on in and around the water. Gradually you become aware that you are not alone.

You look around and are privileged to see the most awe inspiring sight. The pond and all its surroundings are alive with the activity of the elementals. You can see the water being cleaned by kyhils, the air 'hoovered' by esaks, and fairies and imps working very hard to maintain the soil complexity in this damp environment. It is amazing to see. You know you are not visible to them as they have taken no notice of you at all. It is such a breathtaking sight.

Slowly you are aware that your senses have changed. You realise you are feeling as they do. You have an overwhelming desire to heal and support nature and the elements. You know that you will be enlightened if you observe this activity. You choose to do this for many minutes. Eventually, you are guided to return your focus to the pond. Looking at you with the most gorgeous expression is a frog, sitting magnificently on a leaf in the water.

You know it knows you have just been through a particularly enlightening experience. Delightedly the frog turns and hops with a gentle splash into the depths of the pond which makes you smile.

You are so happy you remain by this pond for a little while longer. You reflect on the wonderful elementals which work with and for nature so willingly without question. You are truly humbled by this experience. Slowly you return to your comfortable place knowing your consciousness has again been raised.

Receive a feeling of empathy with the elementals

1. Look at picture (21).
2. Create a little garden, even if it is only in a bowl, dedicated to the fairies and elementals. Make sure you have a little water and lots of greenery in it. You will need flowers if the fairies are to feel included.
3. Invite the fairies and other elementals to visit your garden.
4. Invoke an angel of love and Archangel Michael to protect the elementals.
5. Look after your garden carefully and keep it fresh for the elementals.

Pictures 22 & 23 (Chapter 11) Receive energy from the nature kingdom

Meditation – enlightenment

You find yourself standing next to a geyser and the ground feels alive. You become light-headed and a little out of control as your energy flow has been affected.

You try to ground yourself but are aware of the underground activity. This throws you for a moment and you just do not feel right. With this, the geyser shoots forth its mighty spout of water and it reaches way up into the sky. You are completely in awe of the sight which beholds you. You realise you have come to this spot to re-align, enhance and improve your energy flow. This really excites you.

You are drawn to walk around it but all areas still feel alive and slightly unsafe. However, you reach one particular area and you want to stop. It looks no different from anywhere else really but it gives off the most amazingly powerful energy.

You sit down and cross your legs. You immediately sense the pulse from the Earth's core begin to resonate within you. You start to feel your chi intensify and strengthen. All your chakras expand and fill with the energy and you become acutely aware that it is also pouring into you from above. It appears that this spot is like a 'filling station' and you are glued and unable to move. Every part of your body has become alive. You are excited as the ground shakes again as the geyser prepares to blow. The water pushes from the core of the Earth out into the sky. As the water falls on you the energy from the Earth enters you with an intensity which you have never felt before.

You become very light-headed and no longer connected to your physical body. You realise your aura has expanded beyond your physical frame and it feels wonderful! You begin to sense everything differently and you become aware of so much more than you have ever felt, seen or heard before. It is beyond words. As the geyser subsides you are pressed to breathe deeply and with purpose, ensuring the energy flow from the Earth and the Universe has balanced within you.

With intense urgency you know you must vacate this spot immediately. You get up, walk away and sit on a small hill to observe the geyser from a distance. As you sit there you adjust to your higher vibrational state, which will become the norm for you. You are delighted to have been enlightened. With this you return to your comfortable place ready to receive a new guide who has come to work with you.

Exercise to receive energy and protection from the nature kingdoms

1. Look at pictures (22) and (23).
2. Walk out in nature and call in Archangels Gabriel and Uriel to enfold you in white and yellow light.
3. Feel yourself growing taller as a connection between Heaven and Earth. Know that Archangel Butyalil is shining light on you from above and Archangel Gersisa from below. Feel very loved and protected.
4. Sense your magnificent white unicorn walking beside you. Communicate with him telepathically if you wish to.
5. Then imagine the elementals and spirits who are working all around you to keep everything alive and in divine right order.
6. Send them love and sense they are responding by accompanying you.
7. Feel them protecting you and keeping you safe and happy.
8. When you leave the natural world, thank the Archangels, your unicorn and all the elementals.

Picture 24 (Chapter 11) Receive oneness with nature and the elemental kingdom

Meditation – meet your dragon

You find yourself walking out of a cave into bright sunlight. You are temporarily blinded as your eyes readjust to the light. As you begin to focus again you see a most magnificent, beautiful dragon sitting in front of you.

He is so big and powerful, yet gives you the gentlest feelings. He places his head to the ground, just like a dog would do when wanting to be stroked. You walk over to the dragon and begin to rub his face. His energy is so alive and vibrant, yet re-laxed and at ease. You know you must climb onto his back so you do. You feel very small but completely protected and you know you could never fall off this dragon.

He raises its head and starts to walk around, before stretching his wings to as-cend into the skies. As he flies around, you are aware that he flits from side to side as if avoiding objects and you begin to wonder why he flies this way.

With that your vision changes and you shake your head to try and re-focus again. This, of course, makes no difference as you are now seeing as the dragon sees. Your vision is enhanced and you can now see all levels of the spirit world.

There are colours you have never seen before, a depth that has never been there before and a complete awareness of everything around you. It takes a while for you to get used to this and to take it all in. Your dragon is aware of this and invites you to stay with him for as long as you need to fully appreciate the enormity of the worlds combined.

You accept his offer willingly and stay for as long as you need. You soar to great heights observing and learning from all that you see and encounter. Eventually, he senses when you have learnt all you can during this particular encounter. You find your 'dragon vision' diminishes leaving you to readjust to your usual sight and to reflect on this experience. Your dragon returns you to the ground, where you are able to settle down into your comfortable place enlightened, fulfilled and ready for your next trip with your dragon.

Experience oneness with nature and the elemental kingdom

1. Look at picture (24).
2. Find a place outside in a garden, park or in the countryside where you can be undisturbed.
3. Sense an angel of love enfolding you and Archangels Michael and Metatron standing on either side of you, protecting you and bringing you enlightenment.
4. Sit quietly and sense the flowers and grass growing, helped by the elementals.
5. Be aware of the trees communicating their wisdom and ancient knowledge.
6. Imagine the water sprites playing in the water
7. Feel yourself blending with nature around you. Merge with the trees, flowers or water.
8. Feel that you have become invisible as you become one with nature and the elemental kingdom.
9. Thank them for allowing you to experience their world.
10. Thank the Archangels and angel of love.

Picture 25 (Chapter 12) Receive a sense of welcome and belonging on the spiritual path to enlightenment

Meditation – angel gifts

You find yourself seated on a simple chair within a room. You have no idea where you are but you know that something very exciting is just about to happen. You can't explain why you know, you just do.

As you are thinking about this a door opens and the room is bathed in the colours of the rainbow. You become acutely aware of the presence of angels around you. You are so delighted and happy to be there. Each of the angels has come to welcome you to join them on your journey of spiritual enlightenment and to give you a gift.

One by one the angels come to you and bestow on you their gift. They offer you the opportunity to speak with them about this and what it means for you. You take up this offer with each angel that comes to you. You spend as much time as you need to accept each item they bestow on you and to take in the knowledge shared with you. This is so exciting.

You feel your higher consciousness growing as each gift is understood. As the last angel leaves the room you become aware that your chair is your comfortable place. You are driven to record your experiences and reflect on them over the coming weeks.

Enhance your sense of welcome and belonging on the spiritual path to enlightenment

1. Look at picture (25). First absorb the energy of Kumeka and Archangel Michael in the big Orb over Diana's head. Then let your consciousness take in the angels of love, peace, communication, joy, transformation, enlightenment, protection, hope and purification in this picture.
2. Recognise that each one is welcoming you on the spiritual path to enlightenment.
3. Close your eyes and see a golden path up a mountain in front of you.
4. You are surrounded by guides, angels and archangels as you walk.
5. Everything you see is tinged with love. You know there is a higher reason for everything.
6. Reach the top of the mountain and look round.
7. Know that you belong on this path and the spiritual hierarchy is supporting you.

Picture 26 (Chapter 12) Automatically receive encouragement on your spiritual path

Meditation – progression on your path

You have reached a plateau on your spiritual path and it is beginning to frustrate you a little. You try very hard not to let this negative emotion in, but occasionally you just can't hold it back, so you decide to go for a walk to clear your mind.

You ask for support to move you onwards and upwards on your spiritual path. As you are walking you become aware of a weight in your pocket, which wasn't there a moment ago.

You slip your hand into your pocket and you pull out a crystal. It is a crystal just for you. No one else should touch it. It is yours and yours alone. Immediately as you hold this crystal in your hands, you have an all consuming urge to stop walking and sit down. You find a sunny grassy area to sit down. The sun is warm and full of vibrant energy.

The crystal has started to glow and become translucent in front of your eye. You are able to look into it and as you do this you are met by the most amazing image. It is a vision of you. It shows you exactly what you need to do to step from your plateau and how to progress on your spiritual path. It is so clear and obvious that you know exactly what you must do.

With that your crystal returns to its usual state and you turn to go home with a skip in your step. You know this crystal will remain with you as long as you need it and this gives you confidence and peace.

Returning to your comfortable place you gently enfold your crystal. You smile with delight as you know you are now moving forward on your spiritual path again.

Receive encouragement on your spiritual path

1. Look at picture (26).
2. Feel Archangel Michael placing his blue light of protection around you.
3. Ask any question and know that Kumeka will help you bring the answer to consciousness.
4. Close your eyes and imagine you are going through your next day with Archangel Michael and Kumeka supporting you.
5. The more you envisage this, the more encouragement you receive.

Picture 27 (Chapter 12) Receive a knowing of enlightenment now and an assurance you are on your path

Receive a knowing of enlightenment now and assurance you are on your path

1. Look at picture (27) of Kumeka.
2. Close your eyes and feel his energy entering your third eye and lighting up your consciousness.
3. Now his light is going deep inside you and transmuting your life issues.
4. Feel yourself being held up in the light to receive healing and joy.
5. When you return thank Kumeka.

Picture 28 (Chapter 13) Receive protection from Archangel Michael

Meditation – support for a friend and support for you

You are in a log cabin. A log fire is crackling and it is warm and cosy. You are feeling very snug and ready to bed down for the night. Outside snow is falling very silently. You are sitting at the window looking at the panoramic view which meets your eyes. Everything is silent and covered in crisp white snow and it fills you with a warm peaceful feeling.

Suddenly the phone rings. You take a call from your friend who was out driving when the snow started to fall. Her car has slipped off the road into a shallow ditch. She is quite unnerved and needs to be rescued. You know that you are the nearest person to where she is. She is only five minutes drive away and you decide you must go to pick her up.

You go to your bedroom and put on many layers of clothing and then you set off in your car. The road is very slippery as it hasn't been salted at all. You drive very slowly creeping along at a snail's pace. You begin to get more scared and realise that if you are not careful you too will slip off the road. This would be a disaster.

Suddenly, you become very aware of a blue light shining gently on the road in front of you. The light encloses your car and you know somehow that you are safe. You have no doubt that you will reach your friend. You also know that you will both get back to your home safely. With this understanding the tension within you disappears. You become alert and focused on the job in hand and before you know it you have reached your friend. She is very cold but unharmed and is delighted to see you. She quickly jumps into your warm car. You turn around with ease.

Slowly and carefully you return in your tracks back to your home. When you get home you share with your friend the experience of the blue light. Without question you both know that you were offered high levels of protection. As the two of you warm up in front of the fire you find yourself returned to your comfortable place feeling just great.

Receive protection from Archangel Michael

1. When you are going on a journey or want protection from Archangel Michael look at picture (28).
2. Ask Archangel Michael to protect you during the day or on your specific mission.
3. Know that your request has been received.

Picture 29 (Chapter 13) Receive an awakening to higher powers and protection

This is the experience Kathy's guide, Wywyvsil gave her when she entered this Orb.

As I look into the blue Orb I am pulled deep into it. I am in a very long tunnel. It is close to me, yet not constrictive, and it feels like a very big cuddle. I know that this Orb is extremely powerful. The energy is so vast I just can't find words to describe how far it reaches. I know I am completely protected.

Whilst in the 'tunnel' I am not permitted to see what is round the corner. The tunnel is infinite yet simple. There is no doubt that it will always offer protection should I not rebuff it. It is a little frustrating for me as I can feel so much more but am not permitted to see it. I know it is made of many of these individual 'tunnels.' One for whoever needs it. Even if all of these were used this would not fill even a tiny aspect of this Orb.

Receive an awakening to higher powers and protection

1. Look at picture (29).
2. Close your eyes and let the orb resonate in your third eye.
3. Know that you have connected to Archangel Michael in all his glory.
4. Feel yourself protected.
5. Sense your higher powers being awakened and ask Archangel Michael to activate them when you are ready.
6. Thank Archangel Michael and open your eyes.

Picture 30 (Chapter 14) Receive another level of enlightenment

Meditation – to enlightenment

You find yourself standing in the centre of a maze. The hedges are really high and there is no short cut to the exit. You stand there not knowing which way to go. You try many paths. All of these take you on a journey but not the journey to meet your goal. Eventually exhausted you sit down.

You look to the skies and shout for help to reach your goal. You want to walk your pathway easily and purposefully. You are really frustrated by your lack of progress. Suddenly you are aware of angels everywhere around you. You realise foolishly that all you had to do was ask and be ready to receive their answers. You feel energy enter your crown chakra and move to your heart chakra. This gives you a knowing of where to go and how to leave the maze.

You are inspired, re-energised and with purposeful steps you get up and walk without doubt. As you step from the maze you accept enlightenment and help. You know it is time to return to your comfortable place and walk your path with confidence.

Receive another level of enlightenment

1. Look at picture (30).
2. Say the following invocation to Archangel Gabriel aloud.
3. I now dedicate myself to enlightenment and invoke the mighty Archangel Gabriel to enable me to see everything and everyone with the eyes of spirit.

4. Close your eyes and feel Archangel Gabriel touching your third eye.
5. Relax deeply and allow an expansion of consciousness to take place.
6. Open your eyes and thank Archangel Gabriel.
7. Consciously change your attitude to everything and everyone.

Picture 31 (Chapter 14) Automatically receive purification and healing

Meditation – deep purification

You find yourself in a deep cave. It is full of light from crystals, stalactites and stalagmites, glistening in a variety of different colours. There are thousands so splendid you don't know where to begin to look.

Despite this splendour you are drawn to the back of the cave. It is in darkness. You pick your way through the crystals. Finally you reach the back of the cave and in the far corner there is a certain crystal. It is not like any of the others. It appears quite dull, yet you are compelled to reach forward and touch it. As you do it begins to vibrate.

The vibrations increase in intensity and the crystal begins to glow. It works to remove all negative debris, achieve purification and to raise your consciousness bringing you to the higher dimension. You can feel it focus its energy on your base chakra. As purification is achieved it gives you an emotional release moving you from a feeling of survival to joy.

Now the sacral chakra is engaged. It takes you from a place of pure sexual emotions to an appreciation of both your masculine and feminine sides. As your solar plexus glows in its light you become aware of your own power. It gives purification and you recognise how to use this for the greater good. It feels good to have this greater wisdom. The crystal now works with your heart chakra.

You suddenly feel very emotional a little hurt and unloved. As this chakra is purified you begin to consume an understanding of unconditional love. Your levels of trust are brought into question as it reaches the throat chakra. But as you are purified you sense and recognise your psychic and spiritual abilities.

Focusing now on the third eye the crystal makes you aware of your higher self and of the healing you need. This is provided as this chakra is purified enabling you to reach higher levels of divine inspiration. Lastly, the crystal focuses on the crown chakra which immediately brings forward all past life and soul connection issues. It brings you purification and you are able to link and connect with your true self. With this realisation you continue with higher inspired communication and this is so enlightening.

This is the most powerful purification you have ever experienced as it reaches you on a physical, emotional and etheric level. The crystal continues to glow very brightly. Its energy strengthens your connection with your guide and other divine beings.

When the crystal has finished enlightening you it returns to its quiet state and you find yourself in your comfortable place, truly happy and contented.

Purify yourself

1. Look at picture (31).
2. Close your eyes and relax.
3. Visualise a magnificent waterfall in front of you.
4. Archangels Gabriel and Raphael are with you clothed in white and green light.
5. Imagine yourself taking off your clothes and standing under the water.
6. As you step out into the hot sunshine Archangel Gabriel is radiating pure white light into you. You can feel it penetrating to your core.
7. Archangel Raphael is touching you with emerald green healing light. Feel it entering your cells where it is needed.
8. Feeling pure and shining, put on a white robe and know that healing has taken place at some level within you.
9. With Archangels Gabriel and Raphael walk down a sunny road, feeling happy and light.

You can, of course do this exercise physically when you stand under a shower. Call in Archangels Gabriel and Raphael. Feel the water purifying you and put on white clothes when you are dry again. If you do not have white clothes take a moment to visualise yourself in white.

Picture 32 (Chapter 15) Receive mental release, a sense of peace, and an increase in confidence and help with new beginnings

Meditation – removal of fears and worries

You find yourself walking through dense woods at night and although you shouldn't be scared, you can't help yourself. Every noise makes you jump, even your own footsteps! You know this is silly but you can't shake these feelings. You dig deep and keep walking. Every step you take makes you want to turn and run back out.

But something makes you stay. You don't know what it is or why but you are becoming more confident. With each step you take you feel taller and more significant in the woods.

From the corner of your eye you see a part of the woods shining with light from the moon. It is completely circular and surrounded by trees. This area of complete delight is carpeted with moss and the moonlight highlights its beauty.

You walk over, sit down on the moss and look up at the moon, it is glorious. As you are sitting there you become aware of being protected. You notice that the mossy circle in the trees is now shining a vibrant blue and you are completely bathed in this light.

Gradually, you are aware that you can no longer see the trees or the moon, but this does not bother you. You are relaxed completely safe and totally protected. You know you are not alone and you are surrounded by the love and protection of angels. You are happy and feel safe. You just know you must share with your angels your deepest fears and worries, you know, the ones you never tell another person.

From deep within you want to speak your truths and you hear yourself speak. You know exactly what fear or worry you are sharing but instead of words a bubble containing your truth appears. This is followed by another and another until all your deepest fears and worries are in bubbles floating around you. You are completely relaxed and safe.

You sit there watching each of the bubbles pop and dissolve in front of your eyes; it makes you smile. In the place of the bubbles you see a golden and violet light. Now you know your deepest fears and worries have been transmuted and replaced with opportunities filled with wisdom.

With this they bring to you the illumination to bring these to realisation. This is a wonderful enlightened moment when you know you are protected and that angels will always help you. As this knowing penetrates your whole being, you find yourself back in the woods in the dark.

But now you are skipping happily, humming to yourself, completely confident on your journey. As you reach the edge of the woods you are met with the most glorious sunrise. This allows you gradually to return to your comfortable place, back in your familiar surroundings.

Visualisation to release old mental patterns and find a sense of peace, an increase in confidence and help with new beginnings

It is particularly effective to do this visualisation at the new moon.

1. Find a place where you can be quiet and relaxed and look at picture (32).
2. Close your eyes and imagine you have a heavy basket on your head. It contains all your mental baggage.
3. Notice how it is preventing you from thinking clearly and from fully opening your heart.
4. Ask Archangel Uriel to lift it from you. How do you feel? You now have mental space to change your patterns.
5. Visualise Archangel Uriel's wonderful, yellow-gold Orb, carrying divine wisdom and peace.

6. Mentally tell him you are now ready to access your deepest wisdom to replace the old patterns.

7. Relax deeply to allow Archangel Uriel to start making changes within you.

Picture 33 (Chapter 16) Open to love and a connection with the cosmic heart

This is the experience Kathy's guide, Wywyvsil gave her when she entered this Orb.

As I become enfolded in this Orb I am met by a very simple construction; not complex as I was expecting. I am bathed in its single vibration and given clarity of deep unconditional love from Source. I am told it is we, the receivers, who complicate love, and many of us never fulfil the qualities of unconditional love given to us. This really saddens me.

Meditation – accepting love unconditionally

You find yourself sitting in a meadow, the grass is long and there are many flowers growing everywhere. It is beautiful and you immediately feel your heart chakra glowing. This is unconditional love for the beauty of nature. You close your eyes to take a picture of this scene and to breathe in the fragrance. It holds your heart in such wonderful energy. As you open your eyes instead of the beautiful meadow you are now sitting on the floor of a circular room with every aspect of the room a mirror. All you can see is you.

Every image of you reminds you of all the things you have done in your life, good and bad. These images keep on changing until you reach the image which is today. As you are looking in the mirrors the images dissolve and in their place is a question. 'Do you love yourself unconditionally?' The question disappears and in its place is a pencil waiting for you to write your answer. However, before you have a chance to answer the whole sphere is filled with a very pale pink light.

You know Archangel Chamuel's angels are here to help you. You draw on this energy and the pencil starts to write out your answer. As you read it you can feel your heart chakra gain energy. You know you have unconditional love and enlightenment to take you to a higher level of consciousness. With this feeling and knowledge you return to your comfortable place.

Visualisation to open your heart to cosmic love

1. Find a place where you can be quiet and relaxed.

2. Light a candle and dedicate it to the healing and opening of your heart.

3. Close your eyes and ask your guardian angel to enfold you in a beautiful soft pink cloud of love. You are very safe here. Nothing and no one can hurt you.

4. Ask your angel to show you how you defend your delicate and vulnerable heart. Do you put armour round it, chains, a glass wall or something else? Take your time to recognise your defences.

5. Recognise that this has served you well for a long time but caused you pain.

6. Ask your angel to show you how your fragile and helpless little inner child gets its needs met. Do you become needy, sad or a victim? Does your child sulk and use passive anger? Does it become bolshy and aggressive? Do you please everyone and become a doormat? What else does this vulnerable part of you do, that protects you but holds you back?

7. Acknowledge that this helped you when you were a child but no longer supports you. Are you willing to take your inner child by the hand and act like a wise sensible adult? How differently can you act?

8. Take your inner child by the hand and run lightly and joyfully along the sunny path that leads up the spiritual mountain. Explore it happily.

9. Then place your inner child in your heart.

10. Now open your arms to Archangel Chamuel and let him take you to the cosmic heart.

11. Be very still and listen to the beating of the cosmic heart.

12. When you have finished return to the place where you started and thank your angel.

13. Open your eyes knowing that you can always repeat this exercise and each time you do so your life will become more love filled and joyful.

Picture 34 (Chapter 17) Receive an invitation to the journey to access the stellar gateway

Meditation - grounding

You find you have a very strong urge to become grounded. You don't know why but you know you must achieve this somehow.

You go outside and walk over to the nearest tree. You sit beneath it and this helps, but still the desire within you remains. So you get up and start to walk again, looking for inspiration. You are suddenly drawn to a particular area, you sit down and you realise you are not alone.

Sitting at this spot is a very old man. He is easily a hundred years old, yet he is very fit and agile. He looks up and says to you "You took your time; I have been waiting for you." You are a bit startled by this, but equally intrigued. He goes on to say he knows you need to be more grounded and he has been asked to help you achieve this. You are amazed but delighted with this information.

You sit and wait for him to say something, but he doesn't. Instead he stands up, walks over to you and places his hands on your shoulders. Instantly you are given a very strong energy from the Earth's core into your solar plexus and a vibrant energy from the Divine Source draws down into you. You begin to become aware of your feet. They are now itching with energy and beginning to feel like they are burning. As this feeling intensifies to a level which is nearly too much to bear, the energy redirects to about six inches below your feet.

As this occurs you know you are connected to the Earth and feel more connected to your guide and angels. You realise that something very profound has just occurred. You know you will have to strengthen this connection.

It has opened up an opportunity for you to continue on your path to access the stellar gateway. You now have a much greater passion to ensure all you do is for the greater good and this feels great. With this understanding you return to your comfortable place.

Visualisation to accept an invitation to access your stellar gateway
1. Look at picture (34).
2. Light a candle and find a space where you can be undisturbed.
3. Sit upright with your eyes closed.
4. With your hands in prayer position invoke the mighty Archangel Metatron and see him before you as a shining golden light.
5. Thank him for the invitation to the journey to access your stellar gateway and tell him you accept it.
6. A golden ladder has appeared in front of you and you are climbing up to a magnificent golden ball, your stellar gateway.
7. Enter your stellar gateway.
8. Sit within its glorious light and dedicate yourself in service to the divine. Humbly ask for assistance.
9. When you have finished climb down the ladder and know that you are now on a new path.

Picture 35 (Chapter 18) Receive a feeling of how important it is to look after nature

Meditation – how can you help?

You find yourself in a classroom, along with all your friends. The teacher is presenting a slide show of places on Earth. They are all being damaged by global warming. As you are watching, a particular slide catches your eye. You are compelled to find out more.

Your teacher tells you about the situation depicted in the slide and you are saddened by what you are told. As this is going on your chakras become alert.

They call on this Orb to inspire and inform you. You are told immediately what actions you should take to support the situation. With this, your guide or an angel brings you the tools you need to heal this situation. You have become very keen to take on this task and you spend as long as is needed to complete the healing. Eventually, you are satisfied you have done all you can and you return humbled to your comfortable place.

A prayer for nature

1. Look at picture (35).
2. Offer this prayer. 'In the name of God and all that is light, I ask for the love, strength and resources to help the nature kingdom to flourish. I call on Archangels Purlimiek and the unicorns, as well as the fairies and elementals, to assist me. I dedicate myself to helping and honouring our beautiful planet.'

Picture 36 (Chapter 18) Receive a push to aspire to something better

This is the experience Kathy's guide, Wywyvsil gave her when she entered this Orb.

As I enter this Orb's energy I am compelled to heal the planet. I can feel, taste and sense every aspect of it. I have a strong urge to understand crystals. I want to know how other planets' energy impacts on us. I am drawn to understand how nature nurtures the Earth, in particular water and air. I know I am connected to the heart of the Earth and the infinite Universe. I feel completely stretched. I know that by working with the Orb I can be taken anywhere to acquire knowledge, to work with other beings and gather energies to heal our worlds.

Meditation – let us talk

You are sitting on a grassy hill over-looking the sea. The sun is shining and there is a gentle warm breeze. In the distance you can see something in the sky and it grabs your attention. As it gets closer you realise it is a dragon. It is beautiful and vibrantly coloured. It stops and bows its head, drops its shoulders invitingly, for you to climb on to his back. You are excited and happy to climb aboard.

Once you are sitting comfortably he takes off and soars purposefully towards the sea. He soars at great speed, so you can feel his power and the wind on your face. He then climbs higher into the sky. The energy changes and you realise you are passing through the different realms of the spirit world. Finally as you reach the angelic realms you begin to sense that your vibrations have risen. Eventually, he slows down and stops. He bows again to let you step down.

As you step from the dragon you notice that under your feet the consistency is delicate and spongy. You should feel unsafe, but you don't. You look up and in front of you is a sphere. It looks like glass and you expect it to be solid. But as you walk towards it, you meld into the 'wall' and through into the interior of the sphere. Interestingly, the 'wall' now seems solid. The interior is very large and filled by angels all coming to talk to you. You have no fear and are pleased to be able to talk with them. You spend as long as you need talking with the angels.

They wish you to share all the things you know to be important and to hear what they say. They have much to speak of with you. When you and the angels have finished talking the sphere empties. You are able to walk through the 'wall' again. You look back and the sphere has vanished. You turn your eyes forward and find you are sitting in your comfortable place, fulfilled by your experience of conversing with the angels.

Exercise to aspire to something better

For this you need a pen and paper. Remember you are a magnificent being and all things are possible with pure intention and angelic assistance.

1. Look at picture (36).
2. Write down your highest aspirations for the following year and for your lifetime.
3. Ask Kumeka, the angels of love and your Higher Self to help you.
4. Look often at these aspirations and continue to ask the higher beings to enable you to achieve your highest possible spiritual potential.

Picture 37 (Chapter 19) Receive energy which helps you clarify your vision

Exercise to clarify your vision

Your highest pathway is always one of deep soul satisfaction and joy. One of the reasons we have a physical body is that it acts as a sounding board for your life decisions.

If it seems sensible to train to become an accountant or an electrician but your body feels heavy when you think about it, that is not your divine pathway. On the other hand if the thought of becoming something glamorous makes you feel over excited or ungrounded, that is almost certainly not right either.

Aim for that which lightens you so that you are optimistic, certain and glowing. It should nourish and stretch you.

1. Look at picture (37).
2. Light a candle and ask the unicorns to help you clarify your vision.
3. Write a list of possibilities.
4. Mull over each one in turn, noticing how your body feels. You may like to go for a walk as you do this. You do not have to do it in meditation.
5. When you have clarified your vision you will feel a sense of alignment in your body and soul.
6. Thank the unicorns for the help they have given you.

Picture 38 (Chapter 19) Receive a knowing of innocence and joy

Know innocence and joy

1. Remember what it was like to be a small child when everything was full of wonder. If you cannot remember watch toddlers as they examine a frog or a snail and sense their innocent excitement and joy.
2. Look at picture (38).
3. Take a very slow walk and look at everything with the innocent eyes of a child.
4. Know that Archangel Gabriel comes to you as soon as you are in your essence like this.

Picture 39 (Chapter 20) Receive a whoosh of energy to awaken your heart centre

1. Look at photograph (39).
2. Go and watch a sunrise. Marvel at its beauty and energy.
3. As you look at it rising, raise your arms to honour it.
4. Invoke the angels to awaken your heart centre and fill it with joy, peace and love.

Picture 40 (Chapter 20) Release fear of the unknown

Meditation – motherly love

You find yourself as an unborn baby in the womb. It is warm, snug and very safe. You love it here. You hear every word your mother speaks and her voice vibrates in her energy. You notice every change in her feelings. You can tell if they are physical, emotional or etheric. You sense her chakras every movement and you are completely 'in tune' with her.

Your mother is a very positive person who approaches change and problems as an opportunity. She likes to learn and to achieve that which is for the greater good. You have never experienced any fear. However, you are being forced to move from the womb to your external existence.

For the first time you have a very strange sensation come over you. You are feeling fear and this happens just as you enter the external world. You know this is not right and ask for support to release the fear of the unknown. With this, your mother scoops you up in her arms. This feels so good and you feel really safe again. Every second of every day she continues to reinforce this feeling of security. As you grow older this stays with you and nothing fazes you.

You have no fear of the unknown. You get excited about trying new things and having new adventures. With complete certainty you know you are not fearful of the unknown. Slowly, you become aware that you are sitting in your comfortable chair really looking forward to every day, with confidence and happiness.

Release fear of the unknown

1. Look at photograph (40).
2. Invoke your guardian angel and sense it enfolding you in love and protection. It is transmuting old fears.
3. Invoke Archangel Gabriel's angels to purify your energy.
4. Breathe in Archangel Gabriel's light until it releases your fear of the unknown.
5. Thank your guardian angel and Archangel Gabriel for helping you.

How to recognise Orbs

Each of the Orbs has a signature which can be recognised. However, spirit frequently reminded us to explore them with our hearts not our intellect. Let your intuition tell you who they are.

Generally the nearer an Orb is to you the fainter and bigger it is. For example a distant unicorn is a very bright, small dot, while one who is enfolding you is huge and pale.

The Orbs are all of the angelic hierarchy. The elementals and angels always conduct and protect the spirits of people and animals who have been incarnated on Earth.

Ghosts

These are the spirits of those who have not passed into the light and are stuck in the Earth plane. Each is accompanied by an elemental known as a wuryl. These are usually small, faint, white Orbs without a bright or defined border. They sometimes gather in portals where the energy is lighter and they can receive assistance to pass.

Angels carrying spirits

In our experience these are the most prolific and common of all Orbs. The spirits are people or animals who have passed into the light. When they travel they are accompanied by an angel, which is the Orb. The Orbs can be tiny or large and are invariably present at celebrations because loved ones in spirit want to witness the event. Small ones appear to have a small darker dot within a white circle and are often very close to people or animals.

Larger ones are also white with a defined edge and the face or faces of the spirits being carried often appear as a darker blob. Sometimes the face can be clearly seen and on occasion are recognised by the person they have come to visit.

You can differentiate these from elementals carrying ghosts because the angels are a visible ring round the outside edge.

Very often the angel bringing the spirit will merge with some of Archangel Michael's protective energy so that blue can be discerned in the Orb.

Archangels carrying Masters

When Masters, who have at any time incarnated on Earth travel, they are accompanied by one or more archangels to protect them and hold their energy while they deliver their message. The only exception to this is when a master travels within the golden Christ Light, which is totally protective. When you enlarge one of these Orbs you can often see the master's face quite clearly.

Guardian Angels

These are usually milky white discs, defined but often small and faint. The more help an individual needs, for example if they are feeling uncomfortable in a situation, the closer and larger the Orb will be. They are sometimes seen over a person's ear, talking to them, or over the third eye, protecting them from seeing something psychically or enabling them to see situations or relationships differently.

Angels of Protection

These are milky white discs, similar to guardian angel Orbs but generally larger. They are sometimes seen on the walls of a room that needs to be cleansed, such as a hotel where people of different energies have been using the space. Huge cloudy white Orbs of protection can be seen on houses or forms of transport, holding the energy safely.

Other angels

There are angels of joy, transmutation, peace, happiness, celebration, commitment and many others which look similar to guardian angels; milky white discs. Usually the location will indicate which angel energy they carry. For example, if a room is being renovated you will find angels of transmutation. If there is a celebration you may see angels of joy.

Angels of Love

You can easily recognise these because of their glowing white light. They appear as the brightest of the angels. When an angel of love is witnessing what is happening it is a round white light but as soon as it starts to move you can see its trail. Tiny ones can look like tadpoles while large ones appear as huge rockets. When they zoom round people or animals bringing healing, love and light, they often look like long thin streaks of white light.

These white streaks can merge together into unusual shapes, like flowers or many heads coming from a central ball. They are often oval shaped as they actively radiate healing or protection to elementals, spirits or Masters.

They frequently merge with angel or archangel Orbs and make them appear luminous. They also accompany archangel Orbs as an act of loving service.

Elemental Orbs

Fairies

Fairies look like tiny white pinpricks of light and are often seen in clusters.

Esaks

Esak Orbs are smaller than fairies and often appear as tiny white flakes, found where there has been psychic or physical negativity to clear.

Kyhils

As esaks but they are seen in water.

Imps, elves, and gnomes

These are very rarely seen but are very tiny pinpricks of light.

Pixies

Pixie Orbs look like tiny white circles.

Archangel Orbs

Archangels each work on a colour ray and carry that vibration. The archangel itself is a deep intense colour, while their angels are a lighter shade as they carry less of the energy. The more archangel energy there is in an Orb the deeper and purer the colour.

Some of the archangels also have distinctive patterns. Where archangel energy has merged with another Orb you can usually distinguish the colours or defining patterns.

Archangel Azriel (angel of birth and death)

Archangel Azriel is a shining black.

Archangel Butyalil (looks after cosmic energy round Earth)

Archangel Butyalil is pure white. The chambers within it sometimes look square or oval.

Archangel Chamuel (love)

Archangel Chamuel is a beautiful soft pink as it heals hearts.

Archangel Fhelyai (animals)

Archangel Fhelyai is a golden colour between that of Archangels Uriel and Jophiel. It can be recognised by the ring round the outside for he is contained in pure Source energy. He is also slightly opaque because his energy is so strong that animals need to be protected from the strength of his light.

Archangel Gabriel (purity)

Archangel Gabriel shimmers pure white and distinctive concentric circles can be seen within the Orb.

Archangel Gersisa (looks after the leylines)

Archangel Gersisa is seen as grey. It is an oval shape and at the full moon this shape is extenuated. At the full moon it becomes oval and you can see the ley lines on which it is working, coming to a central point within it.

Archangel Jophiel (wisdom through the crown)

Archangel Jophiel's colour is a pale yellow.

Archangel Metatron (wisdom and ascension)

Archangel Metatron, the mightiest of the archangels, in charge of the stellar gateway, radiates deep gold, through orange and sometimes red.

Archangel Michael (protection and strength)

Archangel Michael is a deep blue. His energy is often seen surrounding other Orbs if he is protecting the being they are carrying or he may be sending protection to a person or place.

Archangel Purlimiek (nature)

Archangel Purlimiek appears as a translucent pale green white.

Archangel Raphael (healing and abundance)

Archangel Raphael is bright emerald green and has concentric circles within his Orb as he radiates healing and abundance.

Archangel Roquiel (Connection with Mother Earth)

This universal Earth angel is black. He is often seen with Archangel Sandalphon.

Archangel Sandalphon (Earth Star)

Archangel Sandalphon is black and white but often appears as grey.

Archangel Uriel (confidence and peace)

Archangel Uriel is deep yellow. If he has been collecting negativity which he has not yet transmuted into light, he can appear brown. You can see the chambers within his Orb which are raised like little rounded pearls. If you cannot see his yellow gold colour you will recognise the shapes.

Archangel Zadkiel (transmutation)

Archangel Zadkiel can be distinguished by his lovely translucent violet light of transmutation.

Seraphim

You can recognise the seraphim by their translucent quality. They are usually alone and shimmer with many pastel colours, predominantly blue.

Unicorns

As with the other Orbs the nearer a unicorn Orb is to you, the bigger and paler is their pure white light. Distant unicorn Orbs are like very bright dots in the sky, much clearer than stars. When they are very close to someone's physical body they are large and a diffuse soft white, unless actively engaged, when they become transparent.

Unicorn Orbs a few feet from a person can be recognised by the distinct white swirling pattern within them.

Transparent Orbs

An Orb becomes transparent if the angel is holding the energy while the person is waiting to respond. I have a picture of my granddaughter running about a play park in high excitement totally oblivious of danger. The guardian angel Orb over her is huge and transparent as it holds the energy while she has the opportunity to assess the situation.

Shapes of Orbs

Round

When an Orb is round it is witnessing a situation and holding the energy for the highest outcome.

Straight sided or concave

An Orb changes shape if it is actively sending out protection or transmitting a particular energy or information. One or all sides may become straight or concave depending on how much it needs to radiate.

Hexagonal

When all six sides of an Orb become straight, so that it is a hexagon, it is fully operational. This can be seen in any type of Orb.

Elongated

Orbs which are moving fast can appear elongated or thin and snakelike. They may have a tail or leave a trail behind them.

Conical or lemon shaped

These are Orbs which are receiving energy directly from the sun or an archangel.

Merged Orbs

When several angels merge together their colours or qualities may be represented within the Orb. If they want to keep their qualities separate their colours will appear in blocks within the Orb.

Glossary of Orbs in this book

Elementals

Elementals are nature spirits, who may belong to fire, air, earth, water or wood. They look after all the different aspects of the natural world.

Fairies

Fairies are nature spirits, about 1ft, or 30cms tall, who belong to the element air and look after flowers. They are mischievous, fun loving, pure and innocent. They work with angels and unicorns. If unicorns add their light to an area, the fairies will remain behind to hold the frequency. There are angels in charge of groups of fairies.

Imps

Imps are only about 1" or, 2.5cms tall – tiny wee beings – so people rarely see them. They are of the combined elements earth, air and water. Their task is to aerate the soil and they work with the pixies. The imps help the seeds to grow. It is they who whisper to a gardener that the seeds need something.

Lyslih

A being from another universe, where there are no angels as we have them, who comes from the heart of God and is on the same frequency level as an archangel. One lyslih is Fekorm, Master of Music.

Pixies

Pixies are earth elementals, smaller than fairies, who look after the structure of soil. Where someone loves their garden the pixies will help get the soil right so ask them to help get the perfect ph. These elementals do not attach themselves to a place but move around. They are trying to help stop soil erosion. Of course they cannot hold the sea back but they can help with the quality of soil when the water has receded. They also work with the bees to help flowers pollinate.

Dragons

Dragons are creatures of the elements. They are wonderful beings with great strength, wisdom, courage, love and they offer protection. They are a companion and once you have been supported by a dragon, that bond will never break. Your dragon will return to you whenever it is needed. They can present themselves as great protectors or as sensitive, loving and gentle depending on your needs.

Esaks

Esaks are new to this planet. They have arrived to help us and also to learn about Earth and life here. They act like vacuum cleaners, sucking up negative energy. If a place needs to be cleansed after a party during which alcohol or drugs are taken, the esaks will arrive to hoover up any lower vibrations left behind.

Kyhils

The kyhils are tiny water elementals whose task it is to hoover up negative energy in the waters of the world.

Elves

Elves are earth elementals who work with trees.

Sylphs

These are air spirits. They are as tiny as a butterfly and their task is to work with flowers and plants. It is through them that the light of the sun can enter the leaves. Sylphs help to keep the air round flowers and plants pure so that they can live in clear energy, which is why you can breathe more freely out in nature. They also assist the flight of birds.

Wuryls

These are elementals assigned to help and hold all stuck souls who have not passed into the light. No one is ever alone.

Gemllia

These are the angelic beings who look after the elementals and are a higher frequency level than guardian angels.

Salamanders

Salamanders are fire elementals, who get out of control when they react to human emotions, causing conflagrations.

Mermaids

Mermaids are water elementals who look after the flora and fauna in the oceans.

Guardian angels

Guardian angels are the lowest of the angelic hierarchy. One is assigned to look after every human. They evolve with their charges.

Angels

There are many kinds of angels who serve and help us. They are a slightly higher frequency than guardian angels. All angels vibrate at the seventh dimension, which is known as the seventh heaven.

Archangels

Archangels are in charge of the angels. There are thousands of them, though only a few who work with humans. We have included Orbs of a few of them:

Archangel Michael

Archangel Michael is one of the best known archangels who work with the blue ray of protection. His Orb is always blue and if an aspect of him merges with another angel or archangel, his distinctive blue can be seen. He gives you strength and courage to face challenges and he will also help you to succeed with your projects. If you are attached to a person, place or situation in a way that no longer serves you, ask him to cut away the negative cords with his sword.

Archangel Jophiel

Archangel Jophiel works with the vibration of golden yellow, and brings you wisdom and illumination. He is in charge of the development of the crown chakra. When you look at an Orb containing his energy he will inspire you and help you connect with divine wisdom.

Archangel Chamuel

Archangel Chamuel is the angel of the heart and resonates with the pink of love. He brings love, compassion and helps people find forgiveness. Where there is pink in an Orb, Archangel Chamuel's energy is there.

Archangel Gabriel

Archangel Gabriel appears as pure white. He brings purification, joy and clarity. So if you look into one of his radiant Orbs you will receive those qualities in your life.

Archangel Raphael

Archangel Raphael is the angel of healing and abundance. He works on the emerald green ray and helps to open up the third eye.

Archangel Uriel

Archangel Uriel is the angel of peace and wisdom. When you look at one of his Orbs you receive confidence and serenity. He will also help you to dissolve your fears.

Archangel Zadkiel

Archangel Zadkiel oversees the Angels of Transmutation who work with the Violet Flame. He also aligns closely with St. Germain the ascended master who accepted the return of the Violet Flame of Transmutation at the Harmonic Convergence in 1987, so that it could be accessed by everyone in the world. This heralded the start of the twenty five year period of purification of the planet leading up to 2012 which is mentioned in the myths of almost every ancient culture.

Archangel Zadkiel is in charge of the soul star, one of the transcendent chakras above the crown. Knowing a little about him will automatically help you to attune more easily to those orbs with his violet light in them and will help you dissolve, purify and transmute elements of your life.

Archangel Metatron

Archangel Metatron is in charge of the Stellar Gateway chakra, which connects us to Source. He works with the Great Pyramid and supervises the karmic records.

Archangel Sandalphon

Archangel Sandalphon is the twin of Archangel Metatron, working with the Earth Star chakra, which is below our feet. It is Archangel Sandalphon who carries prayers to God.

Archangel Purlimiek

Archangel Purlimiek is in charge of nature. Not many people have heard of him and the mighty work he does but he is coming more into prominence now. He works with the cosmic archangels as well as those of the inner Earth. It is he who gives different elementals their various tasks to do. For example they are all working to prevent soil erosion but he would call the pixies in to do a specific job.

Archangel Gersisa

Archangel Gersisa has a feminine energy. She works with Archangels Sandalphon and Roquiel, who help to develop the Earth Star chakra which is below your feet.

Her task is to keep clear the energy round people's Earth Star chakras whether they are spiritually awake or not. This is so that, when you are ready, light can come right through you from Source and start to heal the Earth. She helps to keep the ley lines clear.

Archangel Butyalil

Archangel Butyalil has a masculine force. In the cosmos there are huge currents of energy which affect Earth and he is in charge of keeping these in some sort of balance and synergy round our planet.

In order to do this he works with Archangel Purlimiek and the nature kingdoms and Archangel Gersisa and the earth kingdoms. He communicates with Archangels on other planets. The unicorns are also assisting him with his task as is Archangel Metatron.

Seraphim

Seraphim are the highest of the angelic hierarchy. They maintain God's creation through sound.

Unicorns

At last unicorns are returning to help people on Earth. They bring enlightenment, purity and love to places and individuals. They work with people who have a vision which will help others. Their light is so bright that they have to step down their energy in order to approach you. If they are far away their Orbs appear as small bright spots and as they come nearer, because they have lowered their vibration considerably, their Orbs are very pale, even translucent and much bigger.

Ascended Masters

These are beings who have mastered the lessons of their planets and ascended. Many of these act as teachers in the inner planes. Some who are very well known are Lord Kuthumi, St. Germain, Quan Yin, Mother Mary, Lanto or El Morya. See *New Light on Ascension* by Diana Cooper for more information about the Masters who are currently serving in the spiritual hierarchy. Here is a little about Kumeka and El Morya who appear as Orbs in this book.

Kumeka

Kumeka is a Lord of Light and is currently serving as Chohan or Master of the Eighth Ray. He has never incarnated on Earth but is from another universe where he ascended. Earth has now earned the right to have his presence. He is Diana Cooper's guide and originally she and Shaaron Hutton, with whom she wrote *Discover*

Atlantis, were his only channels. Now he can touch ten million people at any time. His task is to transmute the old and bring enlightenment to the people of Earth.

Wywyvsil

Wywyvsil is Kathy Crosswell's guide. He is a Lord of Light and has never incarnated on Earth. He is from another universe and has recently arrived here to help our planet. He is a Power, a Lord of Karma.

El Morya

El Morya is the Chohan or Master of the first ray, which is red and carries the energy of will, power and action. He is working very closely with the people on the planet to help us with the changes ahead and opportunities for ascension. He is a member of the White brotherhood and originates from Mercury.

Spirit Guides

Everybody has one or more spirit guides. These are the spirits of those who have passed over and gone through training in the inner planes to guide humans. While your guardian angel is assigned to you at birth, your spirit guides are drawn to you according to the level of light you emit. You may have several, all of whom are helping you with different aspects of your life.

Spirits

These are the spirits of those who have passed over. Your loved ones continue to visit you and watch over you. They join you for celebrations and times of mourning. They also travel to continue their own training in the inner planes. Very often they are guided by an angel or archangel and in these Orbs you can see the light of the angelic being surrounding them.

Ghosts

These are the spirits of those who are earthbound after leaving their bodies. They are not alone, for an elemental called a wuryl is assigned to hold them until they see the light. In this book we refer to them as spirits.

List of Orb Photographs

Chapter Two   **Guardian Angels**

Picture 1   Receive courage to speak wisely and hear with understanding.

Picture 2   Receive joy and life force as well as purification and an opening of your consciousness to new opportunities.

Chapter Three   **Children**

Picture 3   Receive energy to work with angels to help your child

Chapter Four   **Angels**

Picture 4   Receive the message that angels support your decisions.

Chapter Five   **Protection**

Picture 5   Receive protection from electrical vibrations.

Picture 6   Receive a feeling of love and protection.

Picture 7   Receive a knowing that the angels look after you when you are out in nature.

Chapter Six   **Clearance and transmutation**

Picture 8   Receive a transmutation of fear to confidence.

Chapter Seven   **Angels of Love**

Picture 9   Receive from the universe a certainty that love is there for you.

Picture 10   Receive an understanding of the unconditional love of animals.

Chapter Eight	**Animals**
Picture 11	Receive unconditional love for you and those you love, from those in spirit.
Picture 12	Receive a desire to connect with animals and the peace this brings.
Picture 13	Receive healing for your soul.
Picture 14	Receive a knowing that humans must expand their consciousness to honour animals.
Chapter Nine	**Sound**
Picture 15	Receive joy and healing.
Picture 16	Receive protection and an understanding of the awesome power of sound.
Chapter Ten	**Spirits**
Picture 17	Receive permission from those in spirit to get on with life.
Picture 18	Receive a direct unicorn connection.
Picture 19	Receive love and healing for yourself and a knowing that your loved ones are receiving it too.
Picture 20	Receive love, protection and enlightenment.
Chapter Eleven	**Elementals**
Picture 21	Receive a feeling of empathy with the elementals.
Picture 22	Receive energy from the nature kingdoms
Picture 23	Receive energy from the nature kingdoms
Picture 24	Receive oneness with nature and the elemental kingdom.
Chapter Twelve	**Guides and Masters**
Picture 25	Receive a sense of welcome and belonging on the spiritual path to enlightenment.
Picture 26	Automatically receive encouragement on your spiritual path.
Picture 27	Receive a knowing of enlightenment NOW and an assurance you are on your path.

Chapter Thirteen **Archangel Michael**

Picture 28 Receive protection from Archangel Michael.

Picture 29 Receive an awakening to higher powers and protection.

Chapter Fourteen **Archangel Gabriel**

Picture 30 Receive another level of enlightenment.

Picture 31 Automatically receive purification and healing.

Chapter Fifteen **Archangel Uriel**

Picture 32 Receive mental release, a sense of peace, an increase in confidence and help with new beginnings.

Chapter Sixteen **Archangel Chamuel**

Picture 33 Open to love and a connection with the cosmic heart.

Chapter Seventeen **Archangels Metatron and Sandalphon**

Picture 34 Receive an invitation to the journey to access your Stellar Gateway.

Chapter Eighteen **Archangels, Purlimiek, Gersisa and Butyalil**

Picture 35 Receive a feeling of how important it is to look after nature.

Picture 36 Receive a push to aspire to something better.

Chapter Nineteen **Unicorns**

Picture 37 Receive energy which helps you clarify your vision.

Picture 38 Receive a knowing of innocence and joy.

Chapter Twenty **Receive Energy from the universe**

Picture 39 Receive a whoosh of energy to awaken your heart centre.

Picture 40 Release fear of the unknown.

Bibliography

Cooper, Diana : *Discover Atlantis*, Hodder Mobius, London, 2005/Findhorn Press 2007 (USA edition)

A New Light On Ascension, **Findhorn Press, Scotland, 2004**

The Web of Light, **Hodder Mobius, London, 2004**

The Wonder of Unicorns, **Findhorn Press, Scotland, 2008**

Websites:

www.dianacooper.com
www.kathycrossswell.com
www.healingorbs.com

THE NEXT STEPS...

Bringing in a wealth of new material on spirit guides, the angelic hierarchy, the powers and the Lords of Karma, the chakras and the archangels as well as the Ascended Masters, this book explains the meaning and importance of the Orbs in a wider context. The book features 48 photographs and meditations with which the reader can experience and absorb the energy of the Orbs more fully and thus accelerate their own ascension path.

Paperback ISBN 978-1-84409-150-8

Diana Cooper and Kathy Crosswell take you on an inner journey, gently but firmly guiding you through four 15-minute meditations each (8 in total), asking you to focus each time on a color photograph of an Orb in the accompanying booklet.

1. Journey to meet an angel of love to fill your heart with joy, compassion, happiness and love and then Archangel Chamuel will connect you to the cosmic heart.
2. Blue Orb meditation with Archangels Michael and Uriel, with a unicorn and the Master El Morya.
3. Receive a boost on your ascension pathway (Orb of Archangels Uriel, Michael, Metatron, Gabriel and Raphael, with Serapis Bey, Paul the Venetian, Lord Meitreya, Mother Mary and spirits).
4. Visit the Great Pyramid so that you can bring forward information from the ancient civilizations of Egypt, Atlantis and Lemuria to assist your ascension pathway.
5. Share in the light and bring forward information from Wywyvsil and Archangel Raphael.
6. Access the light of Archangel Faith, Lord Kuthumi and the Master Imor, to bring you information and opportunity to receive a total trust in your divine connection.
7. Access the light of Archangels Zadkiel, Raphael, Michael, Gabriel, Uriel and the Master Abraham, to bring you information and opportunity to receive a downloading of ancient universal wisdom.
8. Access the light of Archangels Mallory, Uriel and Michael to receive the desire to access your past life wisdom, the protection to do so and the wisdom to use it for your ascension pathway.

Double CD ISBN 978-1-84409-155-3